LEARNING DISABILITIES: WHAT ARE THEY?

Helping Parents and Teachers Understand the Characteristics

Robert Evert Cimera

Rowman & Littlefield Education
Lanham, Maryland • Toronto • Plymouth, UK
2007

Published in the United States of America
by Rowman & Littlefield Education
A Division of Rowman & Littlefield Publishers, Inc.
A wholly owned subsidiary of The Rowman & Littlefield Publishing Group,
Inc.
4501 Forbes Boulevard, Suite 200, Lanham, Maryland 20706
www.rowmaneducation.com

Estover Road
Plymouth PL6 7PY
United Kingdom

British Library Cataloguing in Publication Information Available

Library of Congress Cataloging-in-Publication Data

Cimera, Robert E.
  Learning disabilities : what are they? : helping parents and teachers
understand the characteristics / Robert Evert Cimera.
     p. cm.
  Includes bibliographical references.
  ISBN-13: 978-1-57886-638-0 (hardback : alk. paper)
  ISBN-10: 1-57886-638-3 (hardback : alk. paper)
  ISBN-13: 978-1-57886-639-7 (pbk. : alk. paper)
  ISBN-10: 1-57886-639-1 (pbk. : alk. paper)
  1. Learning disabilities. 2. Developmental disabilities. I. Title.
  LC4704.C56 2007
  371.92—dc22
                                                    2007012882

∞™ The paper used in this publication meets the minimum requirements of
American National Standard for Information Sciences—Permanence of Paper
for Printed Library Materials, ANSI/NISO Z39.48-1992.
Manufactured in the United States of America.

CONTENTS

PREFACE

Before you begin reading the main text, I want to explain a few things about my philosophy of learning disabilities and the terms that I chose to use. You see, many authors view learning disabilities as comprising one large group of individuals who share fairly similar characteristics. Consequently, when researchers write their books, they talk about learning disabilities as a whole and then discuss various strategies that may help one's child or students learn how to read or write or do math better.

I, however, view learning disabilities as several smaller, somewhat related groups of conditions. For example, there are people who have learning disabilities in expressive language, and there are people who have learning disabilities in reading. Although these two groups tend to have certain commonalities (e.g., poor self-esteem and high rates of academic failure), their learning difficulties affect them in distinctive ways. As a result, they usually have unique needs. After all, if a child has a learning disability in reading, she needs to learn how to read. If he has a learning disability in expressive language, he needs to learn strategies that will help him communicate more effectively.

So, in this book, I talk about what learning disabilities are and what characteristics many people with learning disabilities have. I then go into depth about specific learning disabilities. Finally, I conclude with a discussion about preparing all students with learning disabilities for adult life.

When I discuss these various learning disabilities, I use terms such as *dyslexia, dysnomia, dysgraphia, dyscalculia,* and *dysphasia,* the meanings of which have changed considerably over time. Consequently, many academics and researchers no longer use them. However, I do, for three reasons.

The first reason is that it is easier to write *dyslexics* than to constantly repeat the phrase *people with learning disabilities in reading,* or *dysgraphics* for *people with learning disabilities in written language.* In other words, using the names of the specific learning disabilities simply makes the writing easier and, ideally, the reading easier as well.

Second, people are familiar with the term *dyslexia.* It is a trendy and popularized topic. For instance, nearly every high school student knows that Tom Cruise and Cher are dyslexic. So, I believe that many readers would be puzzled if I didn't at least mention it. Yet, if I use the term *dyslexia,* I feel compelled to use the other *dys-* terms as well, at least for the sake of consistency, even though these terms may be considered archaic and technically inappropriate by many academics.

Last, one of my main goals for writing this book is to get parents and teachers to understand that there are many types of learning disabilities and that not everyone with learning disabilities has dyslexia. Dyslexia, although well known, is not the most common type of learning disability. As I discuss at length, most people with learning disabilities can read fine but need help with other academic areas or learning modalities. By including *dysnomia, dyscalculia,* and so forth, I am hoping to drive this point home and get parents and teachers to focus on the learning needs unique to their children and students.

So, there you have it. Now, you know what we will be discussing in this book and why. Let's begin!

1

WHAT ARE LEARNING DISABILITIES?

If you are reading this book, you are probably either a parent or a teacher of a child with a learning disability. Or, maybe, you have a learning disability yourself. At any rate, I should introduce myself and explain why I am writing on this topic.

My name is Robert Cimera. I am a professor of special education at Kent State University. I also have a learning disability. I am writing this book because it has become apparent to me that there is a misunderstanding in the real world about what learning disabilities are and how they affect children. I'll give you an example.

The other day, I was giving a presentation about attention deficit hyperactivity disorder (ADHD) to a group of parents at an elementary school. After I finished, I lingered around talking with anyone who approached me. As I stood in the hallway, about a half-dozen parents came up and began asking me questions. During the course of our conversation, someone mentioned that, in addition to having ADHD, her child also had a learning disability.

Several of the other parents looked sadly at the ground, shook their heads regretfully, and mumbled their apologies. One woman even put her hand on the person's shoulder and said wistfully, "That's okay. Maybe, he could learn a trade like carpentry or work for the city or something."

I was speechless. First of all, this woman made it sound as if it were easy to be a carpenter, which, as my bruised thumbs and rickety fence can attest, it is not! Second, she implied that people with learning disabilities were doomed to a life of ignorance and couldn't become whatever they wanted. According to her, people with learning disabilities couldn't go on to college, get their doctorates, teach at universities, and become successful and happy people.

When I regained my composure, I asked these parents what they thought the term *learning disabilities* meant. Nearly all of them replied with a version of the same notion: "There are kids with mental retardation, and there are normal kids—kids with learning disabilities fall somewhere in between."

Even a day later, I fumed as I thought of these people and how they treated this poor mother. More important, I become sad as I imagined how the child with a "dreaded" learning disability would grow up, believing that he is mildly mentally retarded and can't do anything for himself.

These peoples' views, I have to say in the strongest of terms, are wrong. They are wrong on so many levels that I simply didn't know what to say at the time. As I stood there listening to them, my mouth just kept flopping open like a fish gasping for water. My hands kept gesturing as if I were telling a base runner to steal third.

In the end, I gave the mother my card and begged her to contact me, and I suggested to the other parents that they read an autobiography entitled *The Little Monster: Growing Up With ADHD* (Jergen, 2004). It is about a college professor who has a learning disability and ADHD. Ideally, it will help them understand that people with learning disabilities can succeed in life.

The following morning, I walked into my classroom and began retelling the incident to my students. By then, I had finally found the words that I wanted to say, and I was more than willing to express my frustration to anyone who would at least pretend to pay attention. When I was finished, none of my students seemed bothered by my tale. They just looked at me as if I had written 2 + 2 on the board and proclaimed that the answer was 4. Then, it occurred to me—they believed the same thing! After at least 2 years in our special education program, my students thought that kids with learning disabilities were some how above kids with mental retardation but below so-called normal kids! When I went up and down the aisle asking each soon-to-be teacher whether he or she knew what learning disabilities were, only two students were able to generate answers that were close to the truth—and even these were worthy of only a C-minus at best.

So, here I am, just moments after finishing that class, writing this book. My pulse is still throbbing in my neck from the run up the five flights of stairs that span my classroom and office (or, perhaps, it is throbbing because of my frustration).

Why am I writing? Well, let me tell you as calmly as I can.

I am writing this book for three reasons. The first is to convey to people that having a learning disability isn't like having mental retardation. As I discuss throughout the remaining pages, mental retardation and learning disabilities aren't related in the slightest. Not even a little bit. So please, just forget any preconceived notion that you have about learning disabilities.

Learning disabled doesn't mean stupid. Learning disabilities don't mean that one is dumb or simple or that one can't excel. Kids with learning disabilities can do and be anything that they want to be, at least as much as any "normal" kids can.

I realize that you are probably glancing through these pages looking for something novel or earth shattering. Just in case you don't realize it—you just passed it. The most important thing that I can say to you, the biggest impact that I can have on you and your child or student, lies in the previous two paragraphs. Kids with learning disabilities do not have mental retardation. Furthermore, they can do and be anything that they want to be just as much as kids without any learning problems can.

In fact, in case you didn't know, kids with learning disabilities can have any IQ! They can be perfectly average, below average, and above average. They can even be gifted, such as Albert Einstein, who is thought to have had a learning disability. But I talk about that in greater depth in a couple chapters.

If you cannot understand how important this concept is, let me put it this way: Imagine that you are a little kid again. You are the same as you were all those years ago. But this time, someone in your past, perhaps, the kindergarten teacher whom you always hated, calls your parents and announces that you have a learning disability. Moreover, let's suppose that instead of hearing the word *learning disability*, your parents heard *stupid, incompetent*, or *mentally retarded*. Suppose that your parents believed this and treated you accordingly. I am not saying that they loved you any less; I am just saying that they treated you as if you were all of those things . . . stupid, incompetent, and mentally retarded.

Would your life be any different now? Would you be here reading this book? Would you have the same job that you currently have? Would you be the person whom you are right now at this very second? Probably not.

You see, kids with learning disabilities are limited more by how people treat them than they are by their actual learning problems. In essence, they become what people think they are—slow, stupid, unmotivated, dull . . . add whatever words you like.

If I can get you to understand that children with learning disabilities can succeed and if you engrain into them that they can accomplish anything, just as any other child can, then I have done what I want to do. Again, I cannot understate this point. It is the Holy Grail of education. Teach your child that she can succeed, and she probably will. Teach your child that he is stupid and that he will never make anything out of his life, and he probably won't. It is that simple.

The second reason why I am writing this book is to provide you with basic information about learning disabilities that you might have trouble finding on your own. For instance, I have said what learning disabilities are not. Later in the book, I talk about what they are. I also give you information on how they are diagnosed so that you can determine whether your child was diagnosed correctly.

Finally, I want to provide you with useful strategies on how to teach your child. After all, talking about what learning disabilities are and are not is all well and good, but it doesn't mean much if you don't know how to teach your child the skills that he or she needs to know. So, I go over various strategies, as well as cover skills that are important for succeeding in the adult world nowadays. Last, at the end of the book, I provide tons of resources that can help you learn even more.

Okay, so that is why I am writing this book. Basically, I want to help kids with learning disabilities reach their full potential or accomplish whatever it is that they want out of life. Specifically, I want to help you help your child.

Over the next couple hundred pages or so, I am going to try to give you what you need to know about learning disabilities. Some of it is complex, and I try to go over it in general terms. Again, this is an introductory book, not a graduate-level textbook designed to cover everything in the greatest possible detail. Other information might be a bit boring, so I try to tell you all kinds of silly stories from my personal life and teaching life just to keep you interested, if not to illustrate some sort of salient point.

While you are reading this, picture your child or students. Apply what I discuss directly to them. For example, if I am talking about environmental distractions, picture where your child studies and figure out what things in that environment may be adversely affecting his or her learning. If I talk about issues that don't apply to your child, such as difficulties in math or abstract reasoning, then skim those sections. Again, I want to help. So take what you need, and do what you can with it.

But enough talk about why I want to write this book. Let Dr. Cimera's magical, fun-filled exploration of learning disabilities begin!

WHAT ARE LEARNING DISABILITIES?

The first question that you probably have is "What are learning disabilities, anyway?" That's an excellent one and a brilliant place to start. Let's talk about the definition of *learning disability*.

In past books, I have the tendency to skirt around certain issues. For example, I ask the question "What do you think such and such is?" and then I spend 15 pages giving various historical definitions, illustrating that such and such has changed dramatically over the years, and then I end the section by saying that no one can agree what such and such is. I suppose that it is just part of being a professor. After all, I have to fill a 3-hour lecture somehow!

But let's just cut to the chase and say right up front that there are many definitions of *learning disability*, that few of them agree with each other, and that they tend to change dramatically over the years. I could spend the next 11 chapters quoting philosophers and researchers from antiquity and tell you what they thought learning disabilities were. But in the end, it won't get us to where we need to be to help your child.

So, let's do this. Allow me to talk a little bit about a few things that should help you understand this issue and then discuss what the federal government classifies as a learning disability. Sound good?

Although the historical perspective regarding the definition of *learning disability* doesn't sound important, it will affect you in at least one way. Specifically, if you read or talk to various people about learning disabilities, you will likely become confused. One person might tell you that learning disabilities are one thing. Then, you might watch television and listen to a reporter on a local news show who tells you something different. Your child's teachers might even tell you a third thing. And so forth.

If you listen to and try to reconcile what everyone tells you, you will undoubtedly go mad. So don't. Just relax and accept the fact that there is no universally accepted definition of what a learning disability is. The only definition that you need to be familiar with comes from the federal government. After all, in the end, that is the definition that will affect you and your child the most. So, how does the federal government define *learning disability*?

IDEA's Definition of *Specific Learning Disability*

According to IDEA (2004), that's the Individuals With Disabilities Education Act (I talk about IDEA in greater length later), the term *specific learning disability* is the following:

> a disorder in one or more of the basic psychological processes involved in understanding or in using language, spoken or written, which may manifest itself in imperfect ability to listen, think, speak, read, write, spell, or do mathematical calculations. (§602.30a)

Wait! There's more. According to IDEA, specific learning disabilities include such conditions as perceptual disabilities, brain injury, minimal brain dysfunction, dyslexia, and developmental aphasia. If you don't know what any of those are, don't fret. I talk about them in a little bit.

But wait. There is still more! According to IDEA, specific learning disabilities do not include learning problems caused by vision or hearing impairments; motor dysfunctions; emotional disturbances; environmental, cultural, or economic factors; or mental retardation.

"Specific" Learning Disabilities

Believe it or not, there is a great bit of information in the past three paragraphs. Let's go through them piece by piece. Let's begin by noting what term the federal government uses: *specific learning disabilities*. It is often referred to as *SLD*, which I personally don't like because a lot of people mistakenly think that it means *severe learning disability*. You see, there is no classification of learning disabilities. It isn't like someone can be labeled with a severe learning disability whereas somebody else can be labeled with a moderate, mild, or borderline learning disability. But let's get back to the topic at hand.

What is so significant about the term *specific learning disabilities*? The word *specific* denotes that there are several kinds of learning disabilities. This notion is supported by the inclusion of an array of potential problems that students may experience, including (according to IDEA) the ability to "listen, think, speak, read, write, spell, or do mathematical calculations."

You are probably thinking, "Yeah, so what? There are various kinds of learning disabilities. Who cares?"

The "so what?" is this. Whenever I go to schools and work with students who have learning disabilities, I regularly find kids who don't know what kind of learning disabilities they have. Moreover, the teachers and parents rarely know either. In fact, during my doctoral program, I conducted research that required me to look through hundreds upon hundreds of student files and reports. I never saw any reference to a specific type of learning disability other than the occasional *dyslexia*.

Again, you are probably sitting there waiting for the anvil to drop, wondering what all of this means and why I think it is so bloody important. Let me explain.

Imagine going to the doctor and saying that you are in pain. Before you can finish explaining where the pain is, the doctor jumps up and says "Aha!" and begins to put bandages on your left foot.

Now, this might be great if it is your left foot that is giving you the problem. But chances are, it isn't. It could be that your head or your stomach or the pinkie on your right hand hurts. Your pain could be coming from any number of places other than your left foot. And if the pain is coming from some other place, would the bandage help you? No. Of course, not.

Yet, this is exactly how many kids with learning disabilities are "helped." They have problems in school. Someone diagnoses them as having a "learning disability." They are put into special education, and no one ever takes the time to learn what specific learning disabilities they have. I give you an example.

I have a graduate student in one of my night classes who teaches middle school students with "learning disabilities." During the course of a conversation she mentioned that she focuses nearly all of her time teaching her students how to read. This puzzled me because I knew that she served over 30 students (which is a lot in special education). It would be really odd to have all 30 kids having problems with reading. It just doesn't work that way. Usually, you have a few kids who have to work on their math skills, a few who need to learn how to write better. Still, others have behavioral issues, such as turning work on time or following directions. To have all of her student deficient in reading was just strange. I asked her how that happened.

She looked at me, obviously as puzzled as I was, and said, "What do you mean?"

I explained that it was odd to have 30-some kids with learning disabilities who all had problems learning to read. She became even more perplexed.

"Why?" she asked. "They all have learning disabilities." She said this last part loud and slow so that I could understand what she was saying. "That is what we teach kids with learning disabilities."

To make a very long story short, this teacher (and the other teachers in her school) believes that all kids with learning disabilities have difficulty learning to read. So that is what she teaches them . . . whether they need it or not.

Again, I realize that you probably aren't familiar with learning disabilities yet. After all, you are only a few pages into this book. But you will have to take my word for the fact that not all kids with learning disabilities have reading problems. Some have problems with expressive language or math or writing or whatever.

My learning disability, for instance, involves receptive language. I have problems processing what I am told. I don't have a hearing loss. I am not deaf. I can hear fine. I just can't process auditory information as quickly as when I read something. But I talk more about that later.

My point is this: Most of this teacher's students were getting little out of their education. Most could probably read fine. But because their teacher thought that the term *learning disability* equaled problems with reading, she was wasting valuable time.

Look, perhaps, I am beating a dead geranium (I like horses), but I can't underscore this point enough. It is one of the reoccurring themes of this book. There are many types of learning disabilities, and there is considerable variation between them. If you are going to help your child, you will need to find out what specific learning disability he or she has and then address it appropriately.

If you don't know about different types of learning disabilities or what type your child has, don't worry—by the end of this book, you will. Plus, you will have a host of strategies for helping him or her.

One or More Psychological Processes

The second component of IDEA's definition of *specific learning disabilities* that I want to discuss is the phrase "one or more psychological processes." As with the word *specific*, this phrase indicates that learning disabilities can manifest themselves in a number of ways. Furthermore, it is possible to have a learning disability that affects multiple areas. For instance, your child might have difficulty with reading (dyslexia) as well as writing (dysgraphia).

Imperfect Ability

IDEA's definition of *learning disabilities* also includes the phrase "imperfect ability." Now, whenever I discuss this with my college students, at least one of them gets all wigged out about the "perfect" part of "imperfect." They get upset because they believe that no one is "perfect"; therefore, everyone has a learning disability. Don't overthink this as much as my students do. All that IDEA is saying is that people with learning disabilities have problems in certain areas, including their ability to "listen, think, speak, read, write, spell, or do mathematical calculations."

You are probably wondering, "How 'imperfect' do these abilities have to be for someone to have a learning disability?" That is a great question.

Fortunately, I cover it when I describe how learning disabilities are diagnosed, in chapter 3. So, hang in there.

The Inclusions

IDEA also identifies several conditions included under the "learning disabilities umbrella." These include perceptual disabilities, brain injury, minimal brain dysfunction, dyslexia, and developmental aphasia. Allow me to discuss each in turn.

Perceptual disabilities. When you hear the term *perceptual disabilities*, you might think of hearing impairments or blindness. But that isn't what we are talking about at all. People who can see or hear perfectly fine can still have learning disabilities.

Perceptual disabilities are conditions that make it difficult for a person to comprehend something in a certain way. For example, imagine that you are lying on a grassy hilltop looking at the clouds with a group of your friends. One of your friends points upward and says, "Look! That cloud looks like a three-legged armadillo with a cowboy hat."

You look, but you can't see a three-legged armadillo with a cowboy hat or anything of the sort. You see a leprechaun with four arms and a radish. However, when you say as much, everyone makes fun of you because the cloud clearly looks like a three-legged armadillo with a cowboy hat (at least, it does to your friends).

It isn't that you have a vision problem. It isn't that you are looking at a different cloud. It is just that you perceive the same cloud differently from how everyone around you does. Make sense?

I give you a few more examples. Look at the Figure 1.1. Do you see two faces? Do you see a vase? Do you see a leprechaun with four arms and a radish?

How about the next picture in Figure 1.2? Do you see a young woman wearing a hat and looking over her right shoulder? Or do you see an old woman with a babushka and a wart on her nose?

Let me give you one more example. Have you ever seen the posters with 3-D art? They look like a bunch of multicolored squiggly lines. But allegedly, if you stare through them just so, you are supposed to see a three-dimensional Elvis waving at you or something. Do you know what

Figure 1.1. Perception Test 1. *Source:* **Cycleback.com (2005)**

I am talking about? Those are all examples of how people perceive something differently even though they have 20/20 vision and are all looking at the same thing.

Now, I am not saying that you have a perceptual disability if you can't see the two faces or the old lady or a waving Elvis. I personally cannot see any pictures in three-dimensional posters. Frankly, I think that they are all just hoaxes. I think that somewhere an artist is laughing every

Figure 1.2. Perception Test 2. *Source:* **Funch (1995)**

time someone says, "Oh, yeah! There it is. I couldn't see Elvis at first, but now I do."

However, these pictures do illustrate the idea that people do not perceive things in the same way. Furthermore, their inability to perceive what others perceive isn't attributed to a sensory impairment. It is just how their brains work. In other words, some people don't perceive things as do most people because of a disability. Dyslexia is a good example of this point, but I talk about that a little later.

Brain injury. Believe it or not, the inclusion of brain injury as an example of a specific learning disability is controversial in special education. Pointy-head academics such as myself sit around dark taverns wearing tweed jackets with leather elbow patches sipping expensive coffees and vehemently debating whether a brain injury should be included within the definition of *learning disability*. Keep in mind that most of us don't have social lives, so this is how we occupy our free time!

The issue with brain injuries is that they can result in a huge array of impairments. People with brain injuries might lose long- or short-term memory. They might lose the ability to see colors, hear, read, do mathematical calculations, walk, or talk. They might develop behavioral problems or appear as though they have profound mental retardation. It all depends on what part or parts of the brain is damaged and to what degree.

In other words, a lot of researchers think that including brain damage as a potential type of learning disabilities is nonsensical. After all, brain damage can result in anything. It is like saying that an expectant mother may have a boy or a girl. It is true, of course; but, still, it's a useless statement.

Minimal brain dysfunction. Back in the 1960s and 1970s, the term *ADHD* was not yet coined. People who exhibited ADHD-like symptoms were diagnosed with something called *minimal brain dysfunction*. The idea was that kids who were hyperactive, impulsive, and inattentive had slight brain damage, probably caused as an infant is delivered.

However, minimal brain dysfunction is no longer a condition recognized by the American Psychiatric Association. It will probably be removed from the definition of *specific learning disabilities* when IDEA is reauthorized. But we'll see. Such changes are slow in developing.

Dyslexia. I dedicate an entire chapter to dyslexia. So, I won't talk about it much here, other than to say that it is a learning disability that affects reading and, sometimes, writing. People with dyslexia see letters twisted around, moving, blurry, or what have you. The problem isn't necessarily in their eyes; it involves how the brain processes what it sees. Again, I talk about dyslexia in detail in chapter 5.

Developmental aphasia. "Developmental aphasia"—sounds like a great name for an alternative rock band. I can even picture the band members on stage yelling to the crowd, "Hello Wisconsin! We are . . . uh. We are Devel . . . hmmmm? The name of our band is Developmental . . . hmmm . . . you know who we are! Let's rock 'n' roll!"

Developmental aphasia is a term for people who have difficulty recalling words. It isn't that they don't know the words or how to pronounce them, such as *pneumonoultramicroscopicsilicovolcanoconiosis* or *aluminum*; it's that they have the words that they want to say in their heads but can't get them out. They don't have speech problems, as stutters do. They simply can't say the words that they want to say. It is kind of like the "tip of the tongue" phenomenon that we all experience from time to time. At any rate, I talk about this more when I discuss dysnomia, in chapter 8.

The Exclusions

In addition to listing what specific learning disabilities are, IDEA indicates what learning disabilities are not. More precise, according to the federal government, learning disabilities aren't "learning problems caused by vision or hearing impairments, motor dysfunctions, emotional disturbances, environmental, cultural, or economic factors, or mental retardation."

In case you didn't believe me when I said it earlier—learning disabilities are not the same thing as mental retardation. Learning disabilities and mental retardation are completely different conditions. Furthermore, learning disabilities aren't caused by sensory problems (such as vision or hearing impairments), cultural issues, environmental distractions, or behavior disabilities.

Summary of What Learning Disabilities Are

Okay, so you are still probably waiting for a direct answer to your original question "What are learning disabilities?" Let me be exact:

- Learning disabilities are conditions that impede a person's ability to perform certain activities, such as reading, writing, doing math, speaking, or understanding what is said.
- They are not caused by external factors, such as environmental distractions.
- They are not caused by cultural factors, such as a lack of opportunity to learn.
- They are not caused by other conditions, such as mental retardation, sensory impairments, or behavior disorders.
- They are not caused by a lack of motivation to perform well.

Allow me to state these points another way. Suppose that you have a roomful of 100 kids who are having problems learning. Picture them standing by their desks.

Have all of the kids sit down who are having problems learning because they have mental retardation or because they haven't been given an opportunity to learn. These are students who either have low IQs and poor adaptive skills or move around so frequently that they are not in school much. Out of your class of 100 students, they might account for about 10 to 15.

Now, have all of the kids sit down who are having problems learning because they have some sort of sensory impairment. For example, they might be nearsighted or have hearing loss. If they had glasses or hearing aides, they would learn fine. This would probably account for another 10 to 15 students.

Now, have all of the kids sit down who have problems learning because of some sort of emotional or behavioral disorder. These are kids who might be able to learn but have such a hard time regulating their feelings and actions that they miss out on a lot of their teachers' instruction because they are being disciplined. Again, picture a group of maybe 10 to 20 students sitting down.

Now, have all of the kids sit down who have problems learning because of any other disabilities. Maybe they have ADHD and have difficulty concentrating, or they have epilepsy and they keep missing information because they are having petit mal seizures. This will be another 10 to 15 students.

Finally, have all of the kids sit down who have problems learning because of various distractions. Maybe the room is too hot or too cold or too noisy or whatever. Maybe, they have problems at home—perhaps, their parents are getting a divorce. Or maybe one or more of the students is "in love" with the person in front of him or her. Or maybe some are taking drugs or are hungry or tired. For whatever reason, they are not learning as well as they should. This probably accounts for a large chunk of your 100 students, maybe 20 to 30.

What you have left are a handful of kids with learning disabilities. In essence, people with learning disabilities have difficulty learning, but we don't exactly know why. In other words, defining *learning disabilities* is basically a diagnosis of exclusion. If an individual has troubles learning and the reason does not stem from any of the aforementioned (e.g., mental retardation, sensory problems, lack of an education), then that person must have a learning disability.

SUMMARY

You probably aren't very satisfied with my answer to your question "What are learning disabilities?" And you probably have a ton of other questions, such as "What causes learning disabilities?" "Are they inherited?" and "How are learning disabilities diagnosed?" These are good questions, and fortunately, I discuss them in chapters 2 and 3. But for now, let's review what I have discussed thus far.

First of all, learning disabilities don't mean that someone is stupid or has mental retardation. Hopefully, I made myself clear on this point, but rest assured: This point is important, and I state it over and over in the book. Perhaps, it will sink in.

Second, there are many types of learning disabilities. There is dyslexia, dysnomia, dyscalculia, and a host of others, which I discuss in great length. You need to know what kind of learning disability your child has before you can help him or her.

Third, there is no universally accepted definition of *learning disability*. Because you will likely be dealing with schools and special education programs, you should probably pay most attention to IDEA, or the Individuals With Disabilities Education Act.

Finally, IDEA defines *specific learning disabilities* by stating that if a child has difficulty learning and if that difficulty isn't caused by another disability or by external factors, it's a learning disability. It is not a precise definition, but it is the only one that really matters.

2

WHAT CAUSES
LEARNING DISABILITIES?

I always hesitate before discussing the causes of various disabilities. I realize that it is one of the first questions that people tend to ask, which is why I ended up including this chapter. Still, I feel uncomfortable talking about the topic.

Why? Well, first of all, as a researcher, using the word *cause* is taboo. Every time that a researcher says the *c*-word around other researchers, eyebrows raise and glasses of brandy are lowered in anticipation of the rip-roaring, hair-pulling fight that will inevitably break out.

You see, to say that something "causes" something else is an improvable statement. Research *suggests*. It *supports* a hypothesis. It *strengthens* a particular side of an argument. But research never can prove cause and effect. Actually, research can't prove anything!

Why? Because every research project has its flaws and limitations. It is unavoidable. No matter how skilled the researcher is, how he or she selects the study's participants, collects data, or even frames the research question, he or she will create some sort of bias.

Furthermore, all data are open to interpretation. One pointy-head intellectual might look at some stats and figures and say that it means one thing. Another intellectual, with an equally pointy head, will look at the same stats and figures and conclude that it says something completely different.

Moreover, we have been burned too many times in the past. Just think of all the academics who claimed that the earth was flat, that *Titanic* was unsinkable, or that cigarettes were good for you (which was a common assertion, even until the 1960s). We simply do not like to stick our necks out anymore. Don't believe me? Just try to get an academic to commit to any position. It is like talking to a politician.

Second, as researchers, we can't even effectively define most disabilities, so talking about what causes them is rather pointless. After all, if we can't clearly define something, how can we determine what causes it? We can't.

Finally, I hate talking about the causes of disabilities because many parents consciously or unconsciously blame themselves for their children's conditions. I don't know how many times I have been at a party or workshop or someplace where a parent comes up and asks me, "Can such and such cause learning disabilities?" (or mental retardation or ADHD or whatever condition they are interested in).

I always try to bite my tongue, but they look at me with such sad, pleading eyes that I end up feeling compelled to answer them as honestly as I can. This is usually a bad idea given that almost anything *might* cause a learning disability. Notice that I emphasize *might*. Please keep in mind that I *might* look like Tom Cruise if someone's vision was bad enough, if someone had been drinking, or if Tom really let himself go. Again, as you can see, getting a straightforward answer out of a researcher is near impossible.

As soon as I finish saying, "Yes, such and such *might* cause a learning disability" (or mental retardation or ADHD or whatever), the parents change. They stop listening and start mentally kicking themselves. But the pain that they feel is real, and I feel guilty for "causing" it.

However, with all that said, you are probably still interested in knowing what causes learning disabilities. Fine. I can dig that. I think that I would be curious myself if I were in your shoes. So, this is what I am going to do. In this chapter, I discuss what is currently thought to cause learning disabilities. Notice that I said "thought to cause." Everything that I discuss is theoretical and based on the latest research. Please take it with a sizable grain of salt.

If you are not really interested in the etiology of learning disabilities—great! More power to you. This chapter will probably bore you. So either take the night off or skip ahead to the next chapter. The rest of us will catch up in about a half hour.

For those of you remaining, we are going to begin by looking at the brain. Specifically, we are going to examine how it works. I then talk about the numerous factors that *may* result in learning disabilities. Note that I say "may."

UNDERSTANDING THE BRAIN

Let me begin by saying that most empirically based theories agree that learning disabilities are "caused" at least partly by neurological factors. Yes, other factors, such as the environment or learned behavior, might play a role to some degree, which I discuss later. But for most researchers, the chief instigator for learning disabilities is the child's brain.

Before I can explain how your child's brain may be causing his or her learning problems, we must first understand how the brain works, at least in a rudimentary level. Fortunate for you, my oldest brother is a neurologist. He is the "real" doctor in the family. I have just a doctorate. Anyway, this is what he would have told me about the brain, if I had actually asked him.

Neutrons

Believe it or not, all learning begins from outside of our bodies. Why outside? Because that is where all information comes from. We see things. We hear things. We feel, taste, and smell things. Our brain makes sense of it all and learns from the things that we experience. So let's begin our tour of the brain by going to the outer surface of our bodies—our skin.

When we sense something, whether through our eyes, ears, noses, mouths, or little piggies on our left feet, the first thing that happens is that our neurons register that something is out there. Think of neurons as a network of sensors that cover every single millimeter of our bodies. They are like wires that contain three parts: dendrites, the axon, and the soma (Figure 2.1).

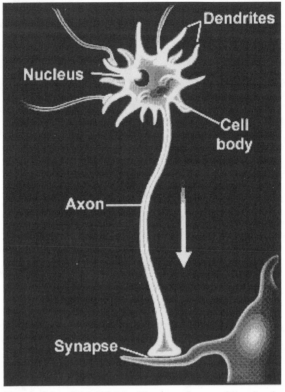

Figure 2.1. The Mighty Neuron. *Source:* **Morphonix (2006)**

The soma, or nerve cell, is the heart of the neuron. It contains the nucleus and other key material. Dendrites are tentacles that receive information and transmit them to the soma. The axon is a long tubelike structure that sends information from the soma to dendrites of other neurons.

Now there is a tiny gap between the axon of one neuron and the dendrites of another. This gap is called the *synapse*. When an electrical impulse, which carries information, gets to the end of an axon, a group of chemicals called *neurotransmitters* are released. The electrical impulse skates across the chemicals and lands on the other side.

Okay, so let's apply all of that. Right now, you are probably holding this book in your hands. The dendrites in your hands are picking up signals that basically say, "Hey, we have a book in our hands!" The dendrites then send this message, in the form of electricity, to the nearest soma, which passes it through its axon.

The electrical message, kind of like your body's e-mail, rushes down the axon and gets to the synapse. But the bridge is out. Oh no! What is it going to do? No worries. The neurotransmitters come to rescue and throw themselves across the synapse so that the electrical message can cross and continue on to the next dendrites, soma, and axon. It goes all the way through the body in this fashion, up the spinal column, and into the brain. Now, the fun begins.

The Brain

The brain consists of several parts, including the brain stem, the cerebellum, and the cerebrum. These can each be broken into many subparts, and those subparts can undoubtedly be subdivided even further. But we won't be going into that kind of detail. I merely want to give you a general overview of your brain and what areas control what actions in your body. Let's begin with the brainstem and then move upward.

The brain stem. The brain stem is located at the base of your head, and it connects the spinal cord to the rest of the brain. It regulates many of the automated behaviors that our bodies need in order to survive, such as breathing and heart rate.

The cerebellum. The cerebellum is located between the brain stem and the cerebrum. It controls many of our motor abilities, such as balance, walking, and posture. It also controls our speech patterns and eye moments.

In terms of size, the cerebellum may be small when compared to the cerebrum, but it is an important part of the brain (as if any part of your brain isn't important). Although it is roughly 10% of the brain's overall mass, the cerebellum contains over half of its neurons. It is a hotbed of activity. As I talk about later, many learning difficulties may be traced to abnormalities in this section of the brain.

The cerebrum. The cerebrum is the largest portion of the brain, and it is shaped like a cooked chicken. Well, it looks that way to me, but that is just how I perceive it (see chapter 1 where I talk about perception). Anyway, the cerebrum contains several regions. For example, it is divided into two hemispheres, the right and the left. It also has four main lobes, including the temporal, the frontal, the parietal, and the occipital.

Each of these regions controls different aspects of your body. For example, if you are right-handed, which 90% of the population is, your left hemisphere controls many skills involving language. Your right hemisphere controls things such as facial recognition and sense of humor. Of course, these areas control other things as well (see figure 2.2). So, let's put all of this together and see if we can tie it to the cause of learning disabilities.

When your body senses something, such as words on a page or someone talking to you, the sensations are transmitted through your body to your brain via the neurons. Various parts of the brain then try to make sense of what the impulses mean.

Many researchers now believe that learning disabilities are caused by abnormalities in certain areas of the brain. For example, people with aphasia or dysnomia (i.e., an expressive language learning disability) are thought to have abnormal Broca and Wernicke areas of the brain, which control speech and comprehension of language.

It isn't that people with learning disabilities have "brain damage" or that their brains are less "evolved" than other people's brains. This isn't the case at all. As I discuss in a little bit, it is just that these areas of the brain don't process information as quickly and accurately as they should.

WHAT CAUSES THESE BRAIN ABNORMALITIES?

Your next question probably involves the cause of these brain abnormalities that apparently result in learning disabilities. Again, I have to restate my discomfort with this topic. First of all, with the majority of cases, we rarely know exactly what causes someone to have a learning disability. So, if anyone ever tells you such and such caused your child to have a learning disability, that person is probably just making things up. Again, we simply don't know.

Second, I am going to talk about several potential causes of learning disabilities. Although a factor such as cigarette smoking during pregnancy might be the cause of one person's learning disabilities, that doesn't mean that it caused a child's learning problems. In other words, if you are reading this in an effort to determine why your child or student has a learning disability, I am afraid that you are going to be disap-

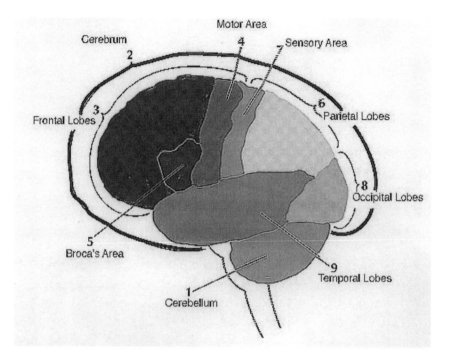

Motor Area

Cerebrum

Sensory Area

Frontal Lobes

Parietal Lobes

Occipital Lobes

Broca's Area

Temporal Lobes

Cerebellum

1. Cerebellum
   - Sits at top of spinal column
   - Controls vital bodily functions
   - Responsible for learned rote movements, such as:
     - playing the piano
     - hitting a tennis ball
2. Cerebrum
   - Holds your memories
   - Allows you to plan
   - Enables you to imagine and think
   - Allows you to:
     - recognize friends
     - read books
     - play games
3. Frontal Lobes
   - Lie directly behind forehead
   - Acts as short-term memory storage sites
   - Responsible for:
     - scheduling
     - planning
     - reasoning
     - imagining
4. Motor Area
   - Helps control voluntary movements
5. Broca's Area
   - Allows thoughts to be transformed into words

6. Parietal Lobes
   - Allow you to enjoy a good meal:
     - taste
     - aroma
     - texture of food
7. Sensory Areas
   - Receive information about:
     - temperature
     - taste
     - touch
     - movement
   - Reading and arithmetic are also functions in the parietal lobes
8. Occipital Lobes
   - Processes images from eyes
   - Links information stored with images stored in memory
9. Temporal Lobes
   - Responds to stimuli such as music
   - Receives information from the ears
   - Underside plays a crucial role in forming and retrieving memories
   - Seems to integrate memories and sensations of taste, sound, sight, and touch

Figure 2.2.   Regions of the Brain and What They Do. *Source: Breitt's Version of Brain Basics* (n.d.)

pointed. I am sorry. I (indeed, no one) can tell you with absolute certainty why your child is the way he or she is.

However, if you want to get a general idea about what the research is currently saying about the etiology of learning disabilities, then I may be of some help. But keep in mind that I talk in generalities and theories, not absolutes. With that said, let's talk about what the research community thinks it knows. Generally, the factors contributing to the brain abnormalities that are thought to lead to learning disabilities are put into four categories: heredity, teratogens, medical factors, and environmental factors.

Heredity

Of the four general areas, heredity is probably the most influential. It is also one of those things that you simply can't control.

Whenever I talk about the genetic component of learning disabilities, mental retardation, ADHD, or whatever, people usually raise their hands and ask, "Who is to blame?" By this, they want to know whether the genetic materials in question are carried by the biological mother or by the biological father. As you might expect, the research is unclear about who carries what genes that lead to learning disabilities. Some studies suggest that maternal DNA is more influential; others insist that the father's DNA is the main culprit. However, in all probability, both parents are responsible at least to some degree.

Teratogens

Teratogens are substances that can cause malformations in an individual's development. Alcohol is likey the most common example. Perhaps, you have heard of fetal alcohol syndrome, which is a condition caused by prenatal alcohol exposure. One of its primary characteristics is mild to moderate mental retardation.

There is a similar condition called fetal alcohol effects. In addition to having delayed physical development, behavior problems, hyperactivity, and attention deficits, approximately two thirds of people who have this condition have learning disabilities. The remaining third are likely to have mild mental retardation.

Although you might not have ever heard of fetal alcohol effects, it is far from being rare. Unfortunately, according to the Centers for Disease Control and Prevention (2006) between 0.6 to 4.5 out of every 1,000 children have fetal alcohol effects. Moreover, this number is increasing substantially. Presently, it is the most preventable cause of learning disabilities.

But alcohol isn't the only teratogen that may cause learning disabilities. Basically, anything that can adversely affect a fetus's development might be responsible, including legal and illegal drugs, cigarette smoke and secondhand smoke, lead, and environmental pollution. Of course, this list isn't extensive, but still, you get the idea.

Medical Factors

Learning disabilities might also be caused by various medical factors, which may or may not be related to heredity or teratogens. For example, premature and low-birthweight babies are at risk for having several conditions, including learning disabilities.

Let me back up. Children are typically in the womb for 40 weeks, or 280 days, and they weigh between 3,000 to 4,000 grams at birth. Of course, these are averages; some children are a little earlier or later or are lighter or heavier. According to the National Center on Health Statistics (2006), approximately 1 out of 10 children is either premature or of low birthweight. Of these, a sizable proportion have learning disabilities, mental retardation, cerebral palsy, or some other disability.

Low birthweight and prematurity usually go hand-in-hand but not always. It is very possible to have a full-term baby who has low birthweight. For example, multiple births, such as twins or triplets, often involve small babies, even if they were in the womb for the full 40 weeks. Furthermore, some children can reach 3,000 grams and be born before the 40th week. My niece was 3,234 grams and born nearly 2 weeks early. She is perfectly fine and doesn't have a learning disability.

There are many reasons why a child might be born early or have a low birthweight. For instance, the first child born to a mother is more likely to be premature or have a low birthweight, as compared to subsequent siblings. Furthermore, young mothers (those under 20 years old) are more likely to have premature or low-birthweight babies than are mothers who are in their mid- to late twenties.

Women who smoke during or just before pregnancy are also more likely to have premature or small children. Some studies suggest that smokers are several times more likely to have low-birthweight or early-born children. Other studies indicate that smoking doubles the chances that a mother will have a child with a cognitive disability (which includes mental retardation and learning disabilities).

But smoking isn't the only factor that increases the risk of prematurity and low birthweight. The mother's diet can also play a role. For instance, women who are obese or extremely thin, such as anorexics, increase their chances of having a child with learning difficulties.

In addition to being born too soon or too small, children who receive poor postnatal care may develop learning disabilities. So, too, can children who have pediatric AIDS or other illnesses.

Environmental Factors

The final category of factors that could cause learning disabilities involves the environment. If you think about it, someone could have a child who is capable of being absolutely brilliant, but because the child was never challenged academically or was brought up in a home without books or educational games, he or she could easily develop learning problems.

PROCESSING

Okay, so what does all of this brain-abnormality information have to do with learning disabilities? Well, it has to do with how people process information. Allow me to explain.

Picture two children. One has a learning disability and the other doesn't. You ask both of them a simple question, such as "What do you want for dinner?"

The "normal" child immediately understands what you have asked and begins processing the answer to your question. She stops and considers what she has a taste for and then tells you, "I want *chana masala!*" (Chana masala is a wonderful Indian dish that I highly recommend. Yum!)

The child with a learning disability in receptive language has a little part of his brain that makes it slightly more difficult for him to understand what he hears. He isn't deaf. He just needs to pay attention a bit more to really comprehend what is being said.

So, the normal child hears a question and understands it and then answers it. The child with a learning disability has to process the question before he can give you an answer. He has to go step-by-step through what you just asked. He might say to himself,

> "What" means that I am being asked a question, so I am expected to answer. "Do you" means that this person is asking something about me, because "you" refers to me. "Want" means my preference for something. "For dinner" means meal. Okay, so she is asking me "What do I want to eat for dinner?"

Now the child with a learning disability can think about the answer. In other words, people with learning disabilities have to take time to process what normal people process instinctively. Consequently, they have twice as much to think about than do people without disabilities. Let me give you another example.

I am going to ask you a question, and I want you to answer it without thinking. Don't think about the question. Just say the first answer that pops into your mind.

What is 2 + 2?

I bet that you answered it right away. You probably didn't even think about what you were saying. I asked what 2 + 2 is, and your immediate answer was 4.

For people with dyscalculia, a learning disability involving math, this problem isn't so ingrained into their brains. They have to think about what each number means and what they should do when they see a plus sign. It isn't that they don't know what a "2" is or what a "+" means; it is just that they have to stop and recall that information from their brains, whereas with you, the information just jumps to your memory. Again, the individual with a learning disability has to process more information that does the non–learning disabled individual.

Furthermore, because of how our brains work, we often don't process certain information as quickly as do other people. Dyslexics have problems

processing the written word. Dyscalculics have problems with processing mathematical formulae. And so on.

So, not only does a person with a learning disability have to process
twice as much as does someone without a learning disability, but the
person with a learning disability will process certain information slower
than the person without a learning disability. No wonder why people
with learning disabilities tend to look as if they are not paying attention
or not trying or why they appear as if they are dumb!

But they are paying attention. They are trying. And they certainly are
not dumb. They just process things differently.

Let's tie this in to what we have learned about the brain. In layper-
son's terms, people with learning disabilities don't process certain stimuli very effectively. It is as if the electrical impulses that carry stimuli
from one's senses to one's brain have to search a bit before they find the
right part of the brain in which to transmit. Then, when it gets there,
that part of the brain has to think harder to understand what it is receiving.

It is much like using an old computer that is crammed with data and
out-of-date software. When you try to find a specific file, its old processing unit (which tends to be a lot slower and inefficient as compared
to newer models) has to look around and around to find where the information is stored. Then, when it gets the information, the out-of-date
software has difficulty making sense out of what has been inputted. See
what I mean? Let me give you one more example about how to understand all of this, and then we will move on.

There are two different ways to think. One way is called *associative
thinking*. Basically, this is how we think about things that we don't
"think" about. For instance, when you drive to work or any place that
you have driven to a number of times, you really don't think about driving. You have done it so often that you don't need to pay attention to
what road you are on or how fast you are driving or that you need to flip
on your turn signal right before you reach such and such street. It is like
you are on automatic pilot. You are so used to driving to this particular
place that you do so more or less on instinct.

As a matter of fact, you might not even remember getting to work or
wherever. You spent your entire car ride thinking about other things.
Rather than focusing on your driving, you were listening to the radio,

singing a song, maybe even drinking your coffee or talking on your cell phone. In other words, driving to work is second nature to you. It requires little active attention.

Cognitive thinking, however, requires far more concentration. You have to focus on each step and actively process everything that is going on before you make an action. This is how we think about new behaviors that we haven't completely mastered.

Again, consider driving. Presently, driving probably involves far more associative thinking than cognitive thinking. You have done it so often that you don't have to actively think about how much pressure to apply to the accelerator or where to turn. However, when you first started driving, it involved far more cognitive thinking than associative thinking. You had to be consciously aware of how fast you were going, which direction to push the gearshift, how to turn on the lights or the windshield wipers, and so forth. Everything was so new that you had to actively process what was going on. Eventually, with practice and exposure to driving, you required far less cognitive thinking. The same is true for math and spelling and many academic areas. You no longer have to actively think about what 2 + 2 is or how to spell *cat*. You have added and spelled so much that it is second nature for you.

Kids with learning disabilities require far more practice and exposure for their learning to become associative. They have to actively think about things more than the typical person does. Furthermore, they have great difficulty carrying on multiple processes at the same time. They have to cognitively think about what is going on, much like a new driver getting behind the wheel. It isn't that they can't get to the same destination as an associative thinking driver—they can. They just have more to process.

ARE LEARNING DISABILITIES PERMANENT?

The final question regarding the cause of learning disabilities that you are probably thinking about is "Are learning disabilities permanent?" The short answer to your question is—no. But this is a qualified no. Let me explain.

As I discuss later in greater detail, according to IDEA, learning disabilities are present only if they affect a student's ability to receive an appropriate education. Technically speaking, it is possible for a student to have a learning disability, be taught how to learn more effectively, thus overcome the inability to receive an appropriate education, and therefore no longer have a learning disability. Unfortunately, this doesn't seem to happen as frequently as it should. You see, special education isn't supposed to be a life sentence. The goal is to teach students what they need to know so that they can function in a typical classroom without supports. But as I have said, this doesn't happen as much as I would like it to.

However, if learning disabilities are caused by differences within the brain, then teaching students how to learn differently will not suddenly correct those differences. Dyslexics can certainly be taught how to read, but various areas of their brain will still be processing visual information atypically. They will still see letters move from time to time.

So, to directly answer your question: No, there is no cure for learning disabilities. But many people are able to learn strategies that will help them process information more efficiently so that they will cease to have problems that distinguish them from others.

Do you see the importance of this point? Please don't sit there thinking glumly, "Darn! I was hoping that my child could get rid of this learning disability thing," because although your child can't be cured in the medical sense, he or she can be educated so that the disability is no longer a problem.

That is why it is so incredibly important for you to make sure that your child gets a good education. That is why you need to get involved in your child's education and make sure that he or she is taught what he or she needs to learn. Ideally, this book will help you do just that.

SUMMARY

In this chapter, I discuss a number of important issues. First, I examine how learning disabilities are thought to be attributed to abnormalities in a person's brain. Furthermore, these abnormalities can be caused by a number of variables, including teratogens and genetics.

Second, I talk about how people with learning disabilities can learn. However, such persons may have to perform far more processing than do those without learning disabilities. They may also have to use cognitive thinking when other people use associative thinking.

Finally, I discuss how the brain abnormalities that result in learning disabilities cannot be cured. Regardless, people with learning disabilities can learn strategies that can help them process information more effectively. I talk about these strategies in future chapters.

HOW ARE LEARNING DISABILITIES DIAGNOSED?

In the first chapter, I discuss what learning disabilities are. More precise, I talk about how IDEA defines *specific learning disabilities* as a term for a group of conditions where one's learning is adversely affected—specifically, in one or two areas, such as in reading, math, expressive language, auditory processing, and so forth.

In the second chapter, I talk about what "causes" learning disabilities. To refresh your memory, researchers really don't know what causes learning disabilities. However, current thought is that learning disabilities stem from differences in how the brain processes information. This isn't to say that people with learning disabilities have defective brains. They don't. They just perceive things differently.

Your next question probably is "So, how are learning disabilities diagnosed?" This is a critical question, especially when considering that, according to a recent newspaper article, one out of four students in special education is misdiagnosed. One out of four! Many of them are mislabeled as having learning disabilities when they actually have something else going on.

In this chapter, I want to talk about how people should be diagnosed with learning disabilities. Ideally, by the end of this chapter, you will be able to determine whether your child has been correctly diagnosed. However, before we begin, I want to talk a little about why children are sometimes diagnosed with learning disabilities when they actually have other conditions.

THE MISDIAGNOSIS OF KIDS
WITH LEARNING DISABILITIES

Whenever I talk about *misdiagnosis*, people seem to automatically attribute the term to incompetent doctors and teachers. But it has been my experience that the reason why many kids are misdiagnosed is not for a professional's lack of competence but out of one's misguided kindness. Let me explain.

Imagine that you are a parent, which is probably pretty easy for you to do. Picture yourself sitting at a table at your child's school with a group of educators and school personnel. Everyone appears sad and uncomfortable. Eventually, the school psychologist opens up a manila folder, glances at a few papers, and then looks at you.

"I am afraid that your child has . . . " the school psychologist pauses for effect, "MENTAL RETARDATION!"

There is a sudden "Daaa-don!" sound in the background as a movie camera zooms in for a close-up of your startled eyes.

Honestly, how would you feel? How would you react? Someone just diagnosed your child with mental retardation. It is a life-changing moment for both you and your child.

It is also a difficult moment for the person doing the diagnosing! Believe me. I hated looking at parents and saying those two words "mental retardation." Parents looked as if I had said "terminal cancer." Many times, they cried. Often, they said that I was wrong, and they cursed me. I even had one father threaten to sue me.

Seriously, hearing a diagnosis of mental retardation is that upsetting! Many researchers equate it with a death in the family. One moment, parents have a happy, healthy "normal" child. The next moment, they have a child with mental retardation. Their hopes of their child becoming a lawyer or doctor or president of the United States disappear. The parents are now faced with something that they hadn't expected. They are forced to look into the unknown and are no longer able to picture their child's future. It really scares the crap out of a lot of people.

What does this have to do with learning disabilities? Take a look at Figure 3.1. Notice anything odd? Do you see the sudden drop in the number of kids with mental retardation? Why do you think that occurred? I give you a hint: It wasn't that we discovered a cure for mental retardation.

Now look at Figure 3.2. See anything odd there? See the juncture where one set of numbers plummet and the other set skyrockets? Wow! Imagine that. Right when the number of kids with mental retardation was miraculously plummeting, the number of kids with learning disabilities was ascending. Hmmm. That must be a coincidence, right? Probably not.

You see, as I have said, it is difficult for teachers and school personnel to look at parents and say, "Your child has mental retardation." It is a gut-wrenching event. In fact, I still can close my eyes and see the faces of many parents to whom I had to say such words. I think, in many ways, that is why I stopped teaching at the precollege level. I simply did not like to deal with that kind of stress.

Other teachers are just like me. They don't like hurting parents either. So what happens? Instead of diagnosing a child with mild or borderline

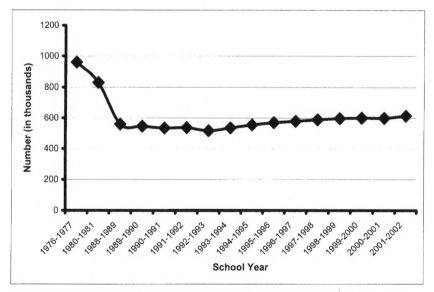

Figure 3.1. Number of Students in Special Education With Mental Retardation (1976-2002). *Source:* **U.S. Department of Education (2002)**

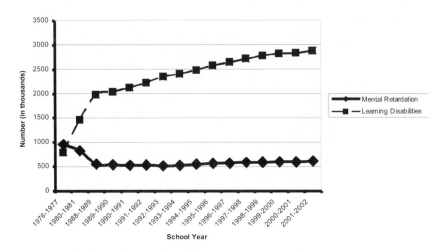

Figure 3.2. Number of Students in Special Education With Mental Retardation and Learning Disabilities (1976-2002). *Source:* **U.S. Department of Education (2002)**

mental retardation, many school personnel will say, "Your child has a severe learning disability." This statement is far less upsetting and anxiety provoking.

Sure, parents still get upset, but teachers are able to respond by saying things like "You know, Albert Einstein had a learning disability." Given this, parents usually perk up a bit, so the teachers add, "So does Tom Cruise, Bill Cosby, and Cher!"

Parents eventually start to think, "Well, hell! If Cher has a learning disability, then it can't be all bad!" And everything seems a little better. And so it goes. In fact, I worked at a school that had an official (although unwritten) policy of assigning a "severe learning disability" diagnosis to every kid with mild or borderline mental retardation. When I asked my director why we did this, he said, "It is less stigmatizing." I never asked whether he meant that for the child, parent, or teacher. I suspect that all three.

THE DIFFERENCE BETWEEN MENTAL RETARDATION AND LEARNING DISABILITIES

In case you don't know, there is no relationship between mental retardation and learning disabilities. None. They are not variations of the same condition. Mental retardation is not a more severe form of a learning disability. The two conditions are completely different. Yes, they are both conditions that hamper learning, but so can blindness and deafness. I hope you get my point.

To really understand the difference, you need to learn a little bit about mental retardation, after which you can compare it to what I have discussed about learning disabilities.

As I examine in the first chapter and at the beginning of this chapter, learning disabilities affect a person's learning in specific areas. For example, dyslexics have problems learning to read. They might also have difficulties with writing. Dyscalculics have problems with mathematics. And so on.

The point is that in most other areas, people with learning disabilities can do fine. A dyslexic can be brilliant at math, and a dyscalculic can be good at reading and writing. People with mental retardation, however, have difficulty in most areas. They have problems in reading, writing, math, and so forth. Moreover, by definition, individuals with mental retardation have to have low IQs and poor adaptive skills (e.g., dealing with changes to their environment).

People with learning disabilities can have any IQ and excellent adaptive skills. People with learning disabilities can even be brilliant, such as Albert Einstein and Cher.

So, please understand that *learning disability* is not a politically correct term for *mild mental retardation*, *dull normal*, *stupid*, or anything like that. People with learning disabilities, such as Albert, Tom, Cher, and myself, can be like everyone else. They simply have different learning needs.

THE STEPS TO DIAGNOSING LEARNING DISABILITIES

With the recent changes to IDEA, understanding the importance of how learning disabilities are diagnosed is crucial. Specifically, the 2004 reauthorization of IDEA strongly emphasizes the process that rules out other potential causes to a student's learning problems. So, let's go through step-by-step how your child should be diagnosed.

Step 1: Someone Notices That There Is a Problem

The first step in the diagnosis of any condition is that someone notices a problem. In the case of learning disabilities, the person most likely to do so is your child's regular education teacher. Most (but not all) students with learning disabilities are identified between the fourth grade and the seventh, depending on the type of learning disability they have.

Students with learning disabilities in reading and written language (dyslexia and dysgraphia) tend to be diagnosed sooner than students with language or math problems (dysnomia and dyscalculia). The reason is that reading and writing are emphasized so much earlier than math. Furthermore, children have a range of language skills, especially early on. So, what is considered "normal" varies considerably. Consequently, children with "abnormal" language skills often go unnoticed until later in life.

Step 2: The Regular Education Teacher Asks for Help

Okay, so your child's regular education teacher notices a problem. Maybe your child isn't learning to read as fast as the others, or he can't do math at his grade level, or she seems to have problems speaking. What happens now?

As soon as the regular education teacher suspects that your child has a disability, that person should talk to the school's special education teacher. The special educator will ask various questions in an effort to figure out what the specific problem is. For example, suppose that your son's regular educator walks up to the special educator and says, "Billy is having problems reading." The special education teacher might ask, "What do you mean? Is he having problems seeing the board? Or are you saying that he doesn't know that *c-a-t* means 'cat'? Or is he having problems saying 'cat' when you show him *c-a-t*?"

Given these initial discussions, the special education teacher should make specific suggestions and recommendations. For instance, if your child's regular education teacher indicates that vision is a problem, the special education teacher might suggest moving your son toward the front of the room and notifying you that he may need glasses.

Step 3: Prereferral Strategies

Okay, let's suppose that the informal recommendations offered by the special education teacher don't help your son learn how to read. In such situations, the regular educator should go back to the special educator and ask for some direct help. The special education teacher will now get more involved. She will come into the classroom and observe what is going on. She might also look at your child's past schoolwork or test results. She may even ask your child some questions.

At this point, the special education teacher should focus on potential external causes of your child's learning problems. That is, she should be looking at how the regular educator's teaching or the classroom environment might be affecting your child's ability to learn.

This is a vital step and, unfortunately, one frequently overlooked. Not every child who has difficulty learning how to read, spell, listen, do math, or whatever has a disability. Believe it or not, many students don't learn because of ineffective teachers or environmental issues, such as sitting near a noisy air conditioner.

Step 4: Referral for a Nondiscriminatory Evaluation

Let's suppose that your child is one of the 30% who are not helped by the prereferral strategies. He may have a learning disability. Of course, he may have any number of other disabilities abilities instead. Or he may not have a disability at all. Maybe he just isn't a good reader. After all, not everyone is gifted in everything.

To find out what is going on, the special education teacher puts together a team who is qualified to give and interpret various assessments. This team is often called an *M-team*, or multidisciplinary team. But it might be called something else in your state, such as *D-team* (diagnostic team), *E-team* (evaluation team), or *PPT* (pupil personnel team).

Regardless, before the special educator can refer your child to the M-team for a nondiscriminatory evaluation, she must first get your permission. If you tell the school that you do not want your child evaluated, the diagnostic process stops right there.

Step 5: Nondiscriminatory Evaluation

For our purposes, suppose that you decided, in writing, to allow the school to conduct a formal nondiscriminatory evaluation on your child. What happens?

The first thing that should happen is that the school will inform you of your rights. For example, you have the right to rescind your consent at any time. If you change your mind and don't want to have your child evaluated, the testing has to stop right then and there.

Next, the school has to tell you, in writing, what is going to happen. It has to tell you what tests are going to be given and by whom. It also has to give you reasonable timelines for completion of the nondiscriminatory evaluation.

You might be wondering, "What exactly is a 'nondiscriminatory evaluation'?" Good question.

A nondiscriminatory evaluation is a systematic effort to collect relevant information that can help determine why your child is having problems learning. It should include several components, including (but not limited to) multiple tests, an extended-period evaluation, a review of past documentation, and medical evaluations.

Multiple tests. Teachers cannot accurately measure your child's abilities with just one test. Why? Well, imagine that your child wasn't feeling well that day or that he or she was distracted by something. That one test probably won't be an accurate measure of your child's ability, and a misdiagnosis could occur. Let me give you an example from my own life.

When I was in second grade, everyone had to take some sort of standardized reading test, the results of which were used to determine what third-grade class we were going to be placed in. The test was pretty high stakes. After all, no one wanted to be in the "slow" third-grade class, with Mr. Wimple. That was the kiss of social death!

I wasn't feeling well the day that we took the test. I had a bad cold or something, which prevented me from concentrating. Consequently, when we got the results back, I saw that I was toward the bottom of the class in reading. My mother couldn't believe it. I had been reading newspapers since I was in kindergarten. So, she made me retake the test after school a few weeks later.

Sure enough, once I was feeling better, I scored toward the top of the class. Had the teachers just looked at the first test, I would have been placed in remedial third grade. Can you imagine what that would have done to my self-esteem, especially when considering that I always loved reading and was fairly good at it?

You really need to make sure that your child is given multiple tests in each area that is being assessed. How many? I would say at least three, although some states mandate only two.

Why three? Because if you take two tests that come up with radically different results, you can't tell which one is the most accurate. With three results, two scores should be close enough that you will have some confidence in concluding that they are correct. In other words, there isn't much of a chance that your child would be equally distracted on all three exams.

An extended-period evaluation. In addition to multiple tests, a nondiscriminatory evaluation should be conducted over an extended period. Doing so makes sure that your child's results weren't biased by something going on in his or her life. For instance, as I write this, I am really sick. I have the flu, I am achy, I have chills. I can't focus my thoughts. If you were to give me an IQ test, I am sure that it would underrepresent my intelligence by as much as 20 points. I am sure that I wouldn't do well tomorrow either. However, if you give me a test next week, when I hopefully feel better, you will probably get a better read on my actual abilities.

Moreover, just imagine if I gave you three tests all in one day. Do you think that you would do as well on the last one as you did on the first? Probably not. You would probably get tired and start making careless mistakes. Again, to get an accurate picture of your child's abilities, assessments need to be spread out a bit.

How far apart should tests be given? There is no magic number; however, I recommend that only one test be given per day and that there be at least one day between tests. But this is just me. Other people have different views on this issue.

A review of past documentation. Okay, so a nondiscriminatory evaluation involves multiple tests given over time. What else? Well, it should also involve a look at past documentation, such the child's class work. This is important because learning disabilities don't suddenly develop. They are thought to exist since birth. As such, there should be some evidence of learning problems early on.

If you look at your child's past work, report cards, comments from teachers, and so forth, you might be able to determine whether your child's problems are new or have always been there in some form or another. Now, it might be that your child never exhibited reading problems before because she is in kindergarten and just started learning how to read. In such a case, she might have a learning disability, but there might not be evidence of it (i.e., from preschool).

However, if your child is in fourth or fifth grade, there should be some indication that problems have existed. Maybe, the first-grade teacher noted that your child was "slow" in learning to write certain letters or read certain letter blends. Again, the point is that learning disabilities just don't spring up. If you find that your child was a superstar speller in elementary school and is now at the bottom of his class in junior high, something other than a learning disability is going on.

Medical examinations. Medical examinations often turn up critical information that can help determine whether a child has a learning disability. For example, many times, when children were referred to me for a nondiscriminatory evaluation, I found out that they didn't have any disability at all but simply needed glasses. In the majority of the cases, my students didn't want to tell their parents that they couldn't see well. They were afraid of having to wear ugly black horn-rim glasses.

I remember one little girl was referred for an evaluation because she was having a horrible time learning how to read and write. She reversed letters and said words out of order, basically displaying many of the symptoms of dyslexia. As a matter of fact, I was convinced that she had dyslexia and was about to refer her to special education.

But her parents took her to an optometrist, who found that the girl had weak muscles in one of her eyes. Consequently, when she was reading and writing, her eyes wouldn't track in unison. She would see things somewhat blurred and jumbled together. It is a long story, but doctors were eventually able to correct the problem. Now, the little girl can read fine.

The moral is to make sure that there isn't anything medically based that could be causing the learning problems. Have your child's vision, hearing, and general health checked out before a final diagnosis is made regarding whether he or she has a learning disability.

Step 6: Referral to Special Education

So, you let the school conduct a thorough nondiscriminatory evalua-tion, and let's say, for the sake of argument, that the M-team determined that your child does in fact have a learning disability that adversely af-fects his education. (I discuss how specifically that diagnosis is made a bit later.) Now what happens?

In most cases, the M-team would probably refer your child to special education. But before your child can get special education services, you have to agree with the team's recommendation. If you don't agree with the recommendation to enroll your child into special education, the process stops here and your child continues to learn in the regular edu-cation classroom without any special services.

If you allow your child to enter special education, you and your child's teachers will sit down and develop what is called an *IEP*, or individual-ized education plan. The IEP outlines exactly what services your child is going to get that school year and what goals he is going to work on. It is an important document, and I talk about it in detail in chapter 11.

Step 7: Reevaluation

Okay, so someone has noticed something different about your child. The teachers have played around with various environmental and teach-ing strategies, but nothing has solved the problem. After being informed about what is going on, you give your informed consent to have your child officially evaluated.

After your child has been assessed and found to have a learning dis-ability and after you agree to enroll your child in special education, an IEP is developed by the IEP team. (Remember, you should be on the IEP team.) Finally, the IEP is implemented and thus evaluated at least every year or whenever needed. But the process isn't finished here.

Every 3 years, or as often as you request, your child must be reevalu-ated. This determines whether he still has a disability that adversely af-fects his ability to get an appropriate education. As I talk about in the second chapter, it isn't uncommon for children to no longer have a learning disability. Ideally, your child's teachers will teach him some use-ful strategies that will improve his learning and thereby end his need for special education.

HOW DO M-TEAMS DIAGNOSE
SPECIFIC LEARNING DISABILITIES?

To ensure that your child has been evaluated correctly by the M-team, you need to understand how specific learning disabilities are identified. Unfortunately, this issue has suddenly become convoluted.

You see, last year, President Bush signed the reauthorization of IDEA. One of the things that make the reauthorization of IDEA so controversial is that it changes how learning disabilities are diagnosed. Specifically, it allows states to decide what definition to use when determining whether a child has a learning disability. So, theoretically and in all possibility, within a couple of years every state in the country will have a policy unlike that of every other state about what a learning disability is and how it is diagnosed.

Before the reauthorization of IDEA, many states utilized what is called the *discrepancy model*. Because this model is probably going to be used over the next few years, at least in a lot of states, I think that it is important that you understand it. However, it is also important for you to check to see what model your state uses.

THE DISCREPANCY MODEL

There are many different ways of diagnosing learning disabilities. Perhaps, the most common involves the discrepancy model, which basically states that a learning disability exists when there is a significant discrepancy between a person's achievement and aptitude and that the discrepancy cannot be explained by any known cause. In other words, the person is not living up to his or her potential, and we don't know why.

You might be asking yourself, "Isn't it kind of presumptuous to say that someone knows what someone else's potential is? Regardless, how is someone's potential measured?"

According to the discrepancy model, someone's potential or aptitude is usually measured in terms of his or her IQ. One's achievement is measured in terms of the work that he or she is able to do. This is usually measured by achievement tests but also by schoolwork.

Okay, so let me show you how this works. But before we begin, I need to give you a crash course on basic descriptive statistics. Specifically, you need to know something about raw scores, standard scores, the bell-shaped curve, and standard deviations.

There is a lot to discuss. So let's get started!

Raw Scores

Raw scores are the actual number of questions that someone gets correct on a standardized test. If your child gets 13 questions correct, her raw score is 13. That's simple enough, right?

Standard Scores

Raw scores are converted to standard scores, which enable people to compare raw scores from different tests. For example, if your daughter got a raw score of 40 on one test and raw score of 53 on a different test, there really is no way to compare these two scores. You can say that she did 13 points better on the second test, but that doesn't really mean anything. After all, one test could have been far easier than the other.

Standard scores convert raw scores into a common currency. It is like taking Mexican pesos and Norwegian krones and converting them to U.S. dollars. Without having a common denomination, you cannot make comparisons.

The Bell-Shaped Curve

If you have taken any kind of introduction to statistics class or psychology class, you probably have seen the mythical bell-shaped curve. Simply put, the bell-shaped curve is a graphic representation of what scientists believe the overall population looks like in relation to certain characteristics, such as intelligence. Look at Figure 3.3. That is an example of a bell-shaped curve.

Each column represents a group of people. The higher the column, the more people in that group. See how the curve bulges up in the middle? That is meant to indicate that most people score in the middle of all possible scores. Likewise, fewer people score really well (to the right) and really poor (to the left). Make sense?

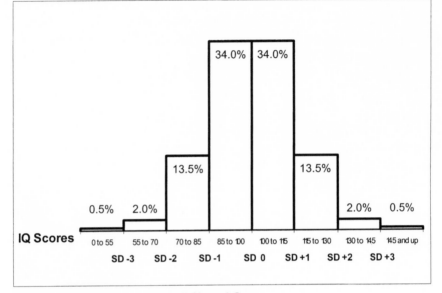

Figure 3.3. An Example of a Bell-Shaped Curve

Okay, the average standard score is 100. So if you get a standard score of 100, you are exactly in the middle of the overall population. Half your friends scored better than you and half scored worse than you. Got it?

Do you see the percentage in each section of the bell-shaped curve? Each percentage indicates the percentage of people who fall somewhere in between the lines. So, roughly 34% of people score a little above the mean (100), and roughly 34% score a little below the mean. As you get farther and farther from the middle, fewer and fewer people achieve those scores.

Standard Deviations

Look at the bell-shaped curve again. See how underneath each column there is an *SD* with a number? Each line represents a standard deviation (*SD*) from the mean.

The standard deviation is the average distance that people scored from the mean score. So *SD 0* is the mean. *SD + 1* is one standard deviation above the mean and *SD – 1* is one standard deviation below the mean. I know that is a lot to wrap your mind around. So just think of standard deviations as boundaries that separate various levels of IQ. This, of course, is a gross oversimplification, but it will do for now.

Now let's start putting everything together. To have a learning disability, your ability or achievement in a certain area (e.g., writing) must be significantly below your overall aptitude, or the level at which you should be performing. Your aptitude can be measured by your overall intelligence, or IQ.

IQs are standard scores. So, if you have an IQ of 100, you have average intelligence. Stated another way, you score as well or better than roughly 50% of the overall population. (Actually, *average* is considered to be within a range from 85 to 115, if that makes you feel any better.)

If you have an IQ of 115, you score as well or better than 84% of the population. See how I am doing that? I am just adding up the percentage of the people to the left of the scores.

Let's suppose that your child has an IQ that is a little above average. Let's say that she has an IQ of 117. You would suspect that she would do comparable work across subject areas. That is, your child should be above average in most academic subjects or at least close to above average. She might be really good at math and score far above the average. Likewise, she might be a little below average in spelling. Still, if she were a typical person, her achievement (what she does in class) should be relatively close to her aptitude (her IQ score).

However, many people have areas that are far below where they should be. For example, suppose that your child has an IQ of 115 but does extremely poorly in reading. Maybe he is failing his classes and gets standard scores of 70 on standardized reading tests. In other words, he isn't "living up to his potential" in reading. This could indicate that he has a learning disability.

Notice that I said that he "could" have a learning disability. Certainly, there are other possible explanations. For example, my beautiful and wonderful wife did poorly in school. Her IQ is well over 130, but she tended to fail her assignments and get below-average grades in her classes. Why? Because she didn't care! She wasn't living up to her potential, because she wasn't trying.

Keep in mind that when I talk about all of these aptitude and achievement test scores, I am presuming that they represent what they are supposed to represent. That is, I am presuming that they are valid, which isn't always the case. If your child isn't trying, if there is something that is distracting him, if she isn't feeling well that day, or whatever, then the test results should be thrown out and you should ask to have your child retested.

Now comes the important part. Remember when I said that the discrepancy model states that learning disabilities could exist when there is a significant discrepancy between aptitude and achievement? Well, let's talk about what *significant* means.

A significant discrepancy is different in every state. So you will need to check with your state's department of education. Check its website. It probably has a link to "special education terms and definitions." Make sure that you bookmark that link; you will probably be referring back to it throughout your child's education.

At any rate, in my state, a student must be below potential by 1.75 standard deviations (recall that the columns presented in the bell-shaped curve are each 1.0 standard deviation). However, other states and definitions of learning disabilities require between 1.5 and 2.0 standard deviations.

I have probably lost you, so let's go back and apply this to your child. Look at Figure 3.4. As I said, we are going to assume that she has an IQ of 115, which is exactly one standard deviation ($SD + 1$) above the average.

Look at her other scores. See where here math score is? It is a little below her IQ, about 112. Moreover, her verbal skills are a little above her IQ, about 120.

Notice how all of those scores are pretty close to where her IQ is? That is typical. Some are a little below; some are a little above. But they are all pretty close.

Now, let's suppose that her standard score in reading is 70. See how far away that is from her intelligence? Her IQ is one standard deviation above the mean, and her reading score is close to two standard deviations below the mean. That is a spread of nearly three standard deviations.

That is really odd. Again, it is reasonable to assume that all of her scores would be near her overall intelligence. So, she might have a learning disability in reading, or dyslexia.

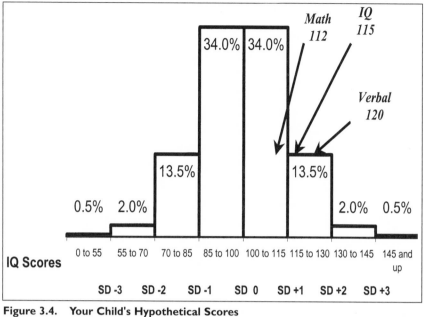

Figure 3.4. Your Child's Hypothetical Scores

Of course, there might be other explanations as well. For example, maybe she doesn't speak English, or she is a nonnative English speaker. Perhaps, she has a vision problem. Maybe she was tired or sick or in love with the person next to her or distracted by something else. All of these could explain why she did so poorly on a reading test.

How can you determine whether low scores are caused by a learning disability or by some other condition or situation? This is an excellent and imperative question. Let's spend some time discussing it.

DETERMINING WHETHER LOW SCORES ARE THE RESULT OF A LEARNING DISABILITY

Let's assume that your child has been tested and that the psychologist found a significant discrepancy between your child's aptitude and achievement in one or two areas. Before you jump to the conclusion that your child has a learning disability, you should consider many things.

Is the Person Qualified to Assess Your Child?

The first thing that you have to ask yourself before you can determine whether your child has a learning disability is "Is the person assessing my child qualified?" To me, this seems like such a logical question. However, few parents ever seem to consider the qualifications of the people assessing their children. Just because someone is employed by a school district doesn't mean that he or she is qualified to determine whether your child has a learning disability.

Generally speaking, you want to have the school psychologist administer and interpret most of the standardized assessments. There are a few tests that can be given by the special education teacher, but that person should at least have a master's degree if he or she is going to be the one completing the assessment report. Moreover, the people diagnosing your child should have recent experience in assessing children. If they haven't conducted an assessment before or haven't done so in a long time, ask for different evaluators. They should also have recent experience with the tests they are giving. Believe it or not, giving standardized tests is not easy. It takes practice. Whenever a new test or a new version of an old test comes out, evaluators need time to get used to it. Otherwise, they may not give it properly.

Speaking of tests, make sure that the tests aren't too old. If they are more than 10 years old, they probably shouldn't be used. If the evaluators use nothing but outdated tests, they probably shouldn't be allowed to assess your child.

Are the Assessment Devices Any Good?

Imagine going to see a doctor about an irregular heartbeat. Instead of using a stethoscope, the doctor puts a rubber chicken on your chest and says, "Funny, I don't hear anything wrong!" How confident would you be in that doctor's diagnosis?

The same issue applies to having your child diagnosed with a learning disability. If the evaluator pulls out a rubber chicken, take that diagnosis with a large grain of salt. Of course, it doesn't have to be a rubber chicken. You should be skeptical of diagnoses made with any bad assessment devices.

How can you tell if an assessment device is bad? Well, as I said earlier, you want to make sure that the assessment devices aren't too old. You see, tests get out of date and are frequently updated and revised. Again, follow the 10-year rule: If a test is more than 10 years old, then it is too old to use.

Moreover, a lot of tests out there are used to diagnose learning disabilities that probably shouldn't be used. How do you tell which should be used? Well, look at the test questions. If they have nothing to do with the student's actual abilities, such as how to read or write or do math, then they really don't tell you much. Let me explain.

There are many tests out there that are used to "diagnose" a learning disability by asking questions such as the following:

"Does your child appear to have problems with mathematical problems?"

"Does your child reverse letters when writing?"

"Does your child do better in some subjects than others?"

Although these questions are certainly important and should be asked at the beginning of any assessment process, their answers do not confirm or refute a diagnosis of learning disabilities. To determine whether your child has a learning disability, someone will have to measure his or her actual abilities. This is the only way to tell whether your child is having difficulty in a certain area.

"What about grades?" you might be wondering. "Couldn't you just look at my child's grades? If she is failing reading but getting A's in everything else, wouldn't that be a good indication that she has a learning disability in reading?"

No. Grades don't measure just ability. They measure whether your child gets work done on time, gets along with others, does the work in the way that the teacher wants it done, and so forth. Just because your child is getting subpar grades in one subject doesn't mean that she doesn't know the material. Maybe she just choked on the final exam. Or she didn't really try that hard on the midterm research paper. Or she is distracted by the boy who sits next to her. There could be an infinite number of reasons why a knowledgeable student does poorly in a class.

Do the Tests Actually Measure a Child's True Abilities?

Let us assume that the evaluator is qualified to give the tests. Let us also assume that the tests are really good. They are up-to-date and top of the line. What else do you have to worry about?

Well, you have to make sure that the tests actually measure your child's abilities. After all, the best, most valid test in the world is only good if the people taking it did their best. What if your child was distracted? Or if he didn't try his best? The results wouldn't mean a thing despite how good the test and the evaluator were. I have a great story that illustrates this point.

I have a friend who is always bragging about her daughter Samantha. She is always saying how BRILLIANT and CLEVER Samantha is. My friend just goes on and on. It is very annoying. I am sure you know the type.

Anyway, one day, my friend announces (a little too proudly) that she is going to have Samantha tested for a special gifted program offered at a prestigious private school.

"Not just anyone can get in," my friend says in sort of a smug voice. "They take only the best and the brightest. My Samantha will finally be with other children just like her."

Gag! Well, okay. She is more of an acquaintance than a friend. But still, the story is good.

So, my "friend" hired a psychologist to come to the school and assess Samantha. All the while, the mother kept predicting how well her daughter would do.

"I bet you anything that she is going to score in the upper first percentile," she blathered on. "I just know it."

As it turned out, not only did dear, sweet, brilliant Samantha not score in the top first percentile, but she actually scored below average. In fact, if memory serves me correctly, her IQ (as measured by this test) was close to 75—which is near the *mentally retarded* range.

My friend was shocked, livid, and embarrassed, all at the same time. She was simply beside herself. She didn't know what happened—at least not at first.

You see, the evaluator came to Samantha's school during recess and began administering various tests, which Samantha didn't want to take. Apparently, at some point during the assessments, Samantha asked when she could go outside and play. The evaluator said something to the effect of "when you are done here."

As you can imagine, that didn't inspire Samantha to do her best. She later confessed to missing questions on purpose so that the test would be over and she could go to recess with her classmates.

When my friend found out, she immediately made Samantha retake the test, threatening her that if she didn't do well, she would not be able to play with her friends for the rest of her natural life. When Samantha was retested, her IQ was in the 120s—certainly respectable but not "gifted." To this day, my friend insists that the second test undervalued Samantha's intelligence by at least 10 points. And so it goes.

The point of the story is that even though you have great tests and skilled evaluators, the results of the assessment might not be accurate. There are a million and one things that could be affecting your child's performance. So, in addition to making sure that the evaluator is competent and the tests aren't old, you need to consider a few other things, including the readiness of the child, the effects of the testing environment, and the effects of the evaluators

Readiness of your child. Perhaps, the first thing that you should ask yourself when trying to determine whether the assessments accurately measure your child's abilities is "Was my child ready to take the tests?" By this, I mean, was the child feeling up to it? Was the child tired? Hungry? Unmotivated? That kind of thing.

You know your child better than anyone. If you think that any given day is a bad day for your child, then make sure that the assessments aren't given on that day. Or at the very least, make sure that comparable assessments are given on another day when he is in a better position to do his best.

Effects of the testing environment. In addition to determining whether your child is ready to take the tests, you must also figure out if the environment in which the tests are taken will affect your child's abilities. I have two really good stories that illustrate this issue.

Like every other kid who wanted to go to college, I had to take the SAT when I was a junior in high school. Because I did so poorly in school and had a pretty low grade point average, I had to do well on the test. So, I really tried hard. I studied, got plenty of rest the night before; I even brought extra no. 2 pencils!

Unfortunately, I was taking the test on a Sunday at a junior college that was directly across the street from a church. What made this event unfortunate was that the church was playing John Denver tunes on their steeple bells. All test long, for 4 to 5 hours, I had to listen to "Leaving on a Jet Plane" and "Rocky Mountain High" over and over and over again. It was maddening. As much as I love John Denver, I simply couldn't concentrate.

I ended up getting an 890 on the SAT. I believe an average score is 1100 or something like that. So, needless to say, I didn't do very well. I blamed John Denver. My parents blamed me.

The second story involves the ACT. I did so badly on the SAT that I couldn't get into any colleges, so my parents made me take the ACT. Again, I was motivated to do well. My parents made me enroll in a study skills class, and I took several pre-ACT tests just to get warmed up.

This time, the environment in which I was taking the test was perfectly quiet, that is, until the fire alarm went off. I can't remember exactly how many times the alarm went off. I am guessing about four, maybe five. But basically every hour, someone pulled the fire alarm, and every hour we had to put our pencils down, grab our things, and go outside until the all-clear sign was given.

When I got my ACT test scores, there was a note attached to them. It said that there had been a problem at the testing center and that I was more than welcome to retake the test for free, should I want to. I looked at my score. I got a 32, which is pretty darn good, especially for a kid with a learning disability! As you can guess, I didn't retake the test.

You see, the fire alarms actually helped me. It broke up the test into more tolerable segments. Instead of sitting there for 3 or 4 hours straight, I worked for an hour and then had to go stand outside for 15 minutes waiting for the all-clear signal. I was able to concentrate better on the tests with the breaks.

So, there you have it. Environments can affect how your child does on assessments. I am not saying that you should keep pulling the fire alarm every hour while your child is being evaluated. I am just pointing out that where tests are given can influence the results.

What I generally recommend is that tests be administered in an environment where the student has been before, such as a classroom. However, distractions such as other students and television sets should be kept to a minimum. Furthermore, absolutely quiet environments are sometimes not the best places to take tests. For example, I get distracted by every little creak and groan of the furniture as people fidget. Even the ticking of the clock or the steady, rhythmic breathing of people can derail my train of thought.

Ask your students where they can think best. Better yet, have multiple tests given in different environments.

Effects of the evaluator. Children, as well as some older individuals, will often behave differently when a stranger is around. This is particularly true for young kids who are shy. The mere presence of a stranger who is asking them challenging questions might alter their abilities.

For this reason, many psychologists will sit and play or chat with kids before the actual testing begins. Not only does this calm the children down, but it also gives the psychologists an opportunity to observe children in nontesting circumstances.

If, for some reason, you believe that your child is not comfortable with the evaluator, ask your child why. Maybe the evaluator is too gruff or whatever. Maybe your child is just ill at ease with men or women. At any rate, try to help your child be more comfortable, or get an evaluator with whom your child can work without being distracted.

Does Your Child's Work Reflect Problems?

Another question that you should ask yourself as your child is being evaluated for a learning disability is "Does my child's schoolwork reflect the same problems identified by the assessments?" In other words, if the evaluator says that your child is terrible or good at math, reading, or whatever, does his or her schoolwork support that statement?

Think about this for a moment. Suppose that your child does really poorly on a standardized mathematics test. According to the psychologist, his abilities are well below those of his peers. Yet, he has always gotten A's in math class. What gives?

Well, it could be a number of things. Perhaps, he panicked on the standardized test. Maybe he didn't try, or he felt ill, or he was distracted by John Denver tunes being played on the church bells across the street. Perhaps, he isn't very good in math and gets lots of help in math class. Maybe his teachers tend to give out A's.

The bottom line is that the test results should be indicative of your child's performance at school. If they aren't, something is wrong. For you to determine whether your child has a learning disability, you must have a good idea where his skills are.

So, when you get the results of the evaluation back, check it against your child's schoolwork. Look at his math worksheets, spelling tests, and so forth. Test him informally yourself. Have him read out loud or listen to a bunch of directions, and see how he does. Do whatever you can to make sure you understand your child's abilities.

Is There a History of Problems?

Finally, you need to ask yourself, "Has my child always had the problems identified by the assessment report?" This is a critical question. As I talk about in the first chapter, people don't suddenly develop learning disabilities; however, they might become more prevalent as educational needs change. For example, you probably won't realize that your child has dyslexia until she starts working with letters and words. The same is true for a child with dyscalculia and math.

Still, if children's problems in reading, math, expressive language, and so forth begin after a traumatic experience, such as a divorce or death in the family or a break-up with a girlfriend or boyfriend, then they probably don't have a learning disability. They are probably just having difficulty learning because of what is going on in their lives.

Again, as I talk about in the first chapter, learning disabilities are primarily a diagnosis of exclusion. A learning disability exists when someone isn't learning up to one's potential and there is no explanation for the delay. To get an accurate diagnosis, you have to rule out all other explanations.

NAME THAT LEARNING DISABILITY

Okay, now it is time to play a fun little game that I like to call "Name That Learning Disability." It will help us apply all of the things that we have discussed thus far.

Here is how we play. I give you some information (test scores) on a fictitious student, and I want you to tell me what kind of learning disability, if any, the student has.

For our game, I am going to pretend that a student has been assessed using, among other things, a standardized achievement test. The test is broken into eight subtests:

Basic reading: Measures decoding and sight-reading abilities.

Mathematic reasoning: Measures problem solving involving geometry, measurement, and statistics.

Spelling: Measures ability to spell accurately.

Reading comprehension: Measures the student's understanding of reading material.

Numeric operations: Measures the ability to write dictated numerals and solve basic addition, subtraction, multiplication, and division problems.

Listening comprehension: Measures the student's understanding of what is spoken.

Oral expression: Measures the ability to name targeted words, give oral directions, explain sequential steps, and describe scenes.

Written expression: Measures organization and development of writing.

Student 1: Sammy

Suppose that our first student, Sammy, has an IQ of 103, which is slightly above average (100). Let's also suppose that he received the following standard scores on our assessment:

Basic reading: 105
Mathematic reasoning: 62
Spelling: 103
Reading comprehension: 101
Numeric operations: 58
Listening comprehension: 109
Oral expression: 106
Written expression: 111

Okay, do you notice anything odd? If not, take a look at the spread of scores that Sammy received. They range from 111 in written expression to 58 in numeric operations. That is strange. If you are a visual learner, plot Sammy's scores on the bell-shaped curve presented in Figure 3.3 or 3.4.

You see, Sammy has an IQ of 103; so, generally speaking, his scores should be reasonably close to that. For the most part, they are, except for his scores in mathematic reasoning and numeric operations, which are lower than his other scores by more than three standard deviations. That is a huge difference.

Now ask yourself, "What do the subtests that he scored really poorly on have in common?" The answer is pretty apparent—math.

What is going on here? Well, of course, we can't really say, given that it is only one test; but it seems that Sammy has great difficulty learning math. Assuming that he tried just as hard on the mathematics subtests as he did on everything else, it appears that Sammy has a mathematical learning disability called *dyscalculia* (which I discuss in more detail in chapter 7).

Try another sample student and see how you do.

Student 2: Gwen

Our second victim is Gwen. Let's suppose that she has an IQ of 82 and she earned the following scores on the subtests:

Basic reading: 77
Mathematic reasoning: 80
Spelling: 91
Reading comprehension: 75
Numeric operations: 80
Listening comprehension: 103
Oral expression: 85
Written expression: 77

Do you think that she has a learning disability? If so, in what area? What is "wrong" with Gwen? Keep in mind that a standard score of 100 is considered average. Clearly, she falls well below average in many areas. But does she have a learning disability?

First, look at the spread of her scores. Her high is 103, in listening comprehension. Her low was 75, in reading comprehension. That is a fairly big gap—not huge like Sammy's but still interesting.

Now look at her IQ. Do you see any difference between her IQ and her other scores? Again, IQ is supposed to be an indication of overall intelligence and cognitive ability. Her scores should fall close to her overall intelligence.

So what do you think? Learning disability or not? And if so, in what areas do you think she has a problem?

Gwen probably doesn't have a learning disability. Yes, she has low scores in most of her subtests, but she also has an IQ that is well below average and close to mental retardation. In other words, although she has subaverage ability in reading, math, and so forth, she is living up to her "potential"; that is, she is doing as well as her overall intelligence would predict.

Remember, not everyone can be great at everything. Some people are average. Some are above average. Some are below average. That is okay.

"But what about her listening comprehension score?" you might be asking yourself. There is a big discrepancy between her IQ (82) and her listening comprehension score (103). Doesn't that mean that she has a learning disability?

No, it doesn't. Remember, to have a learning disability, she needs to do significantly worse in one or two areas than what her IQ would suggest. In Gwen's case, she actually scored significantly above her IQ in listening comprehension. In other words, comprehending what is told to her is one of her strengths.

Let's do one more just to drive the point home.

Student 3: Tonya

Tonya has an IQ of 137, which is really, really good! Only about 2% of people have a better IQ than she does. So Tonya is very smart. Here is how she did on each subtest:

Basic reading: 141
Mathematic reasoning: 139
Spelling: 96

Reading comprehension: 129
Numeric operations: 140
Listening comprehension: 125
Oral expression: 129
Written expression: 92

So, what do you think here? Learning disability? No learning disability? If you think Tonya has a learning disability, in what area does it appear to be affecting her?

Tonya probably has a learning disability in writing. Notice where her written expression and spelling scores are in relation to her IQ and other scores? That is a pretty big difference. And even though she scored close to the average person in written expression and spelling, she should be doing better given her overall intelligence.

There is one little caveat that I want to raise here. It is likely that Tonya is doing reasonably well in school, even though she has an apparent learning disability in areas involving writing. After all, her IQ is sky-high. Plus, her "low" scores in writing aren't really that low when compared to those of the average student. I wouldn't be surprised if she was mostly an A student who gets B's or C's in writing.

What I am hinting is that Tonya may technically have a learning disability. However, it may not be affecting her ability to receive an appropriate education. So, although writing doesn't come as easy to her as, say, mathematics or reading, she probably wouldn't be getting special education services.

This isn't to say that people with learning disabilities must have an average or lower IQ to get help from special education. I am not saying that at all. Some of my former students have been just as cognitively gifted as Tonya is, but their learning disabilities were more pronounced. For instance, their scores in written expression and spelling might have been below 60. Consequently, they had great difficulty passing courses that involved writing.

SUMMARY

In this chapter, I talk about how learning disabilities are diagnosed. I stress the importance of making sure that your child is thoroughly evaluated. This means that multiple tests should be given, schoolwork needs to be reviewed, and medical exams must be conducted (e.g., vision and hearing tests). The idea is that you will have to rule out all other explanations for your child's performance before a diagnosis of learning disability can be considered.

Furthermore, before you accept someone's diagnosis, ask a lot of questions. See if the evaluator is qualified. Determine whether that person is using up-to-date tests. Make sure that your child was motivated to do well on the tests that were given.

Diagnosing a child with a learning disability isn't an exact science. There is considerable subjectivity to it, and there are many factors that can throw off the results. So please get involved with the diagnostic procedures, and make sure that the results accurately reflect your child's situation.

4

COMMON CHARACTERISTICS OF CHILDREN WITH LEARNING DISABILITIES

In the first chapter, I talk about how there are many kinds of learning disabilities. One can have a learning disability just in math, called *dyscalculia*; in reading, *dyslexia*; in expressive language, *dysnomia*; and so forth.

In the following chapters, I talk about each of these and several other conditions. As you will see, each learning disability has its own characteristics. For example, dyslexics sometimes see letters as if they are moving around the page. Dysgraphics, however, sometimes have difficulty with their hand–eye coordination.

However, some characteristics overlap the various learning disabilities. For instance, both dyslexics and dysgraphics are likely to have poor handwriting and difficulty in writing. But not all kids with learning difficulties have these issues.

What I want to do in this chapter is cover some of the characteristics common to nearly all children with learning disabilities. Notice that I say "nearly all." A population as diverse as those with learning disabilities is going to have considerable variation in its behavior and outlook. Still, there are a few things that we need to discuss for you to understand your child.

SELF-ESTEEM

Perhaps, the most important characteristic common across individuals with learning disabilities is self-esteem—specifically, low self-esteem. Think about it. If you struggled in school and were different from everyone else around you, wouldn't you have low self-esteem, too?

As someone with a learning disability, I cannot stress this enough. What affected me most in life wasn't my difficulty in learning auditory information. What affected me the most was the feeling that I was a loser.

Even now, with my doctorate, seven or eight books, nominations for numerous national awards, yada, yada, yada . . . even with all of the many wonderful things that I have accomplished, I still feel like the little kid who was constantly made fun of and teased. I still feel like I can't do anything right. Even now, on occasion, I get depressed.

Look, I don't mean to lay all of this heavy stuff on you, and I don't want you to think that I want your pity. I don't. I truly have a wonderful life. But that is just my point. As great a life as I have, I still feel bad about myself. It isn't that I am a bad person. It isn't that I have done something wrong. It is how I was treated as I was growing up.

I will spare you all of the horror stories. Your child is probably living them as we speak. So for now, let's not focus on my experiences. Let's talk about some general facts and figures. They will probably be of more interest to you.

For example, according to numerous studies cited by Bender (2004), individuals with learning disabilities are far more likely the general population to suffer from clinical depression. Moreover, adolescents with learning disabilities attempt suicide and abuse drugs or alcohol at a higher rate than that of their nondisabled peers. In other words, they tend to self-medicate their problems.

Do I have your attention yet?

My point is that, sometimes, there are more important things to worry about than your child's reading or math ability. I don't mean to scare you. I just want to make sure that you are aware of the side effects of learning disabilities.

So, what can you do address this issue? Good question. After all, we are here to make a difference in your child's life. Strategies for improving the self-esteem of your child can fill an entire book. At the very least, I want to give you a handful of ideas that can get you started.

The first and most important thing that you have to do to increase your child's self-esteem is to make sure that your love isn't tied to anything. That is to say, you should have unconditional love for your child.

Now, I know that sounds like common sense. You are probably sitting there thinking, "Yes, of course, I love my child unconditionally." But my question to you is "Does your child know that?"

Before you say yes again, please consider it from your child's perspective. The view might startle you. Let me give you my own two cents' worth.

Deep down, I know that my parents loved me. I really do know that. But there were many, many times when I didn't *feel* it. Do you know what I am saying?

My mother in particular would frequently tell me, "Robert, I love you but . . . " She would then go on for a good 5 or 10 or 15 minutes about how I was disappointing her. Either I was doing something that I shouldn't, or I wasn't living up to my potential in school. Or whatever. Does any of this sound familiar?

I am not saying that parents and teachers shouldn't talk to children about their shortcomings. I am not saying that at all. In fact, I think that we should be open and honest with kids. They aren't good at everything, and that is okay.

What I am saying is that there should be a balance. No, strike that. There should be an overwhelming number of times that you say something positive about your child. The scale should be tipped so much that the positive side is on the ground.

Again, maybe you think that you already do this. And maybe you do. However, if your child has poor self-esteem, what could a little more praise hurt?

There are several guidelines for giving your child both praise and criticism. For example, praise must be honest. Believe it or not, kids aren't stupid. They can see through you pretty well. If you start saying things like "Hey, you did a great job during today's game!" when your child struck out every time that he was at the plate and dropped every ball thrown to him, he is going to know that you are blowing smoke.

Second, praise has to be consistent. You can't be on your child's back all semester long for getting low grades and then say, "Hey, a D-minus isn't bad. At least you tried. That is what is important." If trying is what was important, then you would have been stressing trying rather than getting good grades. Can you see the inconsistency there? It is subtle, but your kids can pick up on the hypocrisy.

Third, explain why you are proud, happy, or whatever you are feeling. As perceptive as children can be, they may not understand why you are praising them. I have a story about that from my own life.

My father was never the type of man to give compliments. As a matter of fact, I can remember only one time that he ever said that he was proud of me. We were in a big fight. I was yelling. He was yelling. And, for some reason, through my tears, I screamed, "You never say that you are proud of me!"

My father yelled back, "Of course, I am proud of you!" But when I asked why, he couldn't give a reason. He hemmed and hawed and finally said, "Because you are my son."

That reason never satisfied me. It was a stupid, shallow answer, and my father knew it. He stormed off in a big huff that was probably designed to mask his embarrassment.

My father died 5 months ago. All of my brothers stood up at the funeral to tell stories about him. I didn't. The only thing that I could really remember with any clarity was his inability to find one thing, one little thing, for which he was proud about me. So please, make sure that your child knows why you love him or her.

Fourth, praise children for something that they can control. You don't want to say, "Hey, good job on the weather!" After all, they had no part in making the sun shine or clouds rain.

As for giving criticism, emphasize the behavior or outcome that you don't like—not the children themselves. For example say, "I don't like it when dishes get broken" rather than "I don't like you when you misbehave" or "You make me really upset when you break things."

Second, your criticisms should be as neutral as possible. Again, you aren't attacking your child. You are merely pointing out that you don't appreciate something or that some area needs to be improved.

Also, your criticisms shouldn't be emotional. Even if you are trying to be helpful, your comment probably won't sound that way if you have a raised voice or your body language shows that you are annoyed or upset. So, if you have to give a criticism to your child, do so when you are in a fair mood. Even if you think that you can master your anger or disappointment, it will probably show through in how you hold your hands, purse your lips, or wrinkle your forehead.

Finally, all criticisms should be part of a discussion. This means that you should give your child equal time to explain his or her point of view. Perhaps, there is a reason why things turned out the way that they did. Maybe the dish was already broken. God knows that I got blamed for plenty of things that my brothers did. If my parents would have just listened to me before they started yelling, they would have found that out.

Another way to help children with learning disabilities build their self-esteem is to introduce them to kids with similar problems. For example, have them join support or study groups for people with learning disabilities. By being around people who have faced the same ordeals, children can begin to see that they aren't losers or alone.

Moreover, encourage your child to learn about people who have learning disabilities and have succeeded, such as those featured in Table 4.1, all of whom have or had learning problems. Maybe there is someone on this list that your child looks up to or appreciates. By understanding that others have overcome similar problems, children might begin to believe that they can do the same.

Finally, encourage children to focus on the things that they can do well. I am not saying that they shouldn't try to improve their weak areas.

Table 4.1.   Famous People With Learning Disabilities Who Have Succeeded

Magic Johnson	Beethoven	Woodrow Wilson
Eddie Rickenbacker	Charles Schwab	Henry Winkler
John F. Kennedy	Cher	Whoopi Goldberg
Harry Belafonte	Danny Glover	F. Scott Fitzgerald
Bruce Jenner	Gen. William Westmoreland	Tom Cruise
Jules Verne	George Bernard Shaw	Alexander Graham Bell
Steve McQueen	Greg Louganis	Louis Pasteur
Carl Lewis	Hans Christian Anderson	Robert Jergen
Tom Smothers	Henry Ford	Dwight D. Eisenhower
Walt Disney	John Lennon	Robin Williams
Albert Einstein	Nelson Rockefeller	Galileo
Suzanne Somers	Robert Kennedy	Lindsay Wagner
Thomas Edison	Sylvester Stallone	Mozart
George C. Scott	Winston Churchill	Werner von Braun
Gen. George Patton	Wright Brothers	Leonardo da Vinci

Source: Child Development Institute (2006)

I am just saying that they should not forget the fact that they are probably good at many things.

SOCIAL SKILLS

Several researchers have found that people with learning disabilities tend to have poor social skills. This is probably the result of their feeling different and becoming isolated from peers more than it is from the actual learning disability itself. Moreover, it is probably one of the leading causes of why kids with learning disabilities are frequently depressed.

So, how can you help your child build effective social skills? Well, there are many ways. For example, you could role-play certain social situations so that your child can practice how to interact with peers. There are also social skills curricula that you can buy online or at your local teacher resource store. However, the most effective way to teach children social skills is to encourage them to interact with other children. Specifically, you should promote interactions with other children who behave appropriately. The last thing you want is your child developing worse social skills!

Try to get your child to participate in clubs, sports, or group activities. This is a good way for them to meet people who share similar interests. Moreover, structured environments can help children figure out how they are supposed to behave.

You might want to have your child start off in small groups, with maybe one or two other kids. This is especially appropriate if your child has severe anxiety when being around new people or situations. You can always gradually increase the number by adding a new person here and there.

Again, the idea is to provide children with frequent exposure to positive social interactions. This will help them practice their social skills as well as reduce their anxiety about being in social situations.

RISK TAKING

Imagine that you have a learning disability and that nearly every time you raise your hand in class, the answer that you give is wrong. Moreover, imagine that your peers tend to chuckle at you and that your teachers tend to roll their eyes or send you out of the room or give you big fat F's on all of your papers. After several years of trying, what do you think will eventually happen to you?

If you were like most kids with learning disabilities, you would eventually just give up. After all, why should you take a chance on being wrong? That is why most individuals with learning disabilities aren't risk takers.

But this lack of risk taking won't affect just their desire to volunteer answers in school. Many people with learning disabilities will also have difficulty taking risks in other areas of life. For instance, they might not attempt to go to college, because they don't think that they are "college material." Or maybe they won't go into their desired profession, because they think that they aren't smart enough or that they are just going to fail even if they try. They might not even ask people out on dates because of the risks that are involved.

So, what should you do as a parent or teacher? First of all, encourage children to take risks. Have them explain their opinions on controversial issues or try things that they haven't been successful at before.

Moreover, reward your child's effort, not just her outcome. If your child tries out for basketball but doesn't make the team, focus on the fact that she tried. Same thing if she doesn't get a perfect score on a math assignment. At least she tried and didn't leave any blank.

Finally, encourage your child to dream and to dream big. If he wants to be a professional basketball player or president of the United States, great. Show your support and help him reach those dreams in anyway that you can.

Far too often, parents and teachers are quick to squash the dreams of children with disabilities. I bet that I have heard parents or teachers say, "That's not realistic," maybe 500 or 600 times in regard to a child's dreams. It is so demoralizing.

Even in my own life, I kept running up against the walls that my parents and teachers created. For instance, I once told my high school journalism teacher that I wanted to be a writer. She told me that "it takes a special kind of person to be a professional writer" and that I didn't have "what it takes."

Furthermore, my mother frequently told me things like "You can do anything that you set your mind to, but you never really follow through on anything that you start." And so it goes. No wonder I wasn't very motivated to try new things. I never thought that I could succeed.

Please don't misunderstand me. I am not blaming my parents or teachers. I am a writer and I went to college. However, many of the subtle and not-so-subtle comments really did a number on my self-image and my desire to take risks. The same might be true with your child.

HIGH SCHOOL COMPLETION AND POSTSECONDARY EDUCATION

According to the U.S. Department of Education (2001), approximately 27% of students with learning disabilities either officially drop out of high school or simply stop attending. That is nearly 3 out of 10. Compare this to 11% of the general high school population (National Center for Education Statistics, 2006). Furthermore, of those who graduate, only 27% of high school students with learning disabilities will go on to some sort of postsecondary education, including tech schools, 2-year colleges, and 4-year universities—this compared to 68% of the nondisabled high school population (Sitlington & Clark, 2006).

I know that I am probably preaching to the choir, but those who have difficulty learning are already at a distinct disadvantage in society. They often already feel as if they are failures, and they frequently find themselves isolated from their peers. By failing to graduate college, let alone high school, people with learning disabilities typically condemn themselves to lives in poverty. Just consider the following facts: Someone without a high school diploma can expect to make $609,900 throughout an entire life. An individual with a bachelor's degree, however, can expect to make approximately $1,421,000 (U.S. Department of Labor, 2006). That is a huge difference.

So, what can you do to make sure that your child graduates high school and gets the education that he or she needs in order to succeed? The first step is to simply instill into children the expectation that they will continue their education after they graduate high school. How do you do this? Well, you could do what my parents did.

Despite struggling throughout school, I never once thought that I wouldn't go on to college. Furthermore, the thought of dropping out of high school never occurred to me. I simply grew up with those values. My parents habitually asked me, "What university do you want to go to after you graduate high school?" and "What do you want to do with your life?" Even as a young child, my mother and father always reinforced the idea that I would some day go on to college. We even visited various universities when I entered junior high.

So what else can you do? You have to prepare children for their futures. The desire to go to college wasn't what made me get into and stay in school. I needed to learn how to learn. I needed to learn how to study and take effective notes. Fortunately, my academic advisor at Purdue suggested that I sign up for a study skills class. It is the best course that I have ever taken. I strongly recommend that you have your child take such a course as early in his or her academic career as possible.

Another suggestion that I have is to make sure that all of your child's IEP goals prepare her or him for the future. The goals should be something valuable rather than just busywork. For example, have them focus on academic, study, and self-advocacy skills. If you don't know what an IEP is, you will when you finish chapter 11. But for now, understand that it is a legally binding document between parents and schools that outlines what services are going to be provided to kids with disabilities.

Finally, if you want to prepare your child for the future, don't forget about nonuniversity options, such as community colleges, trade schools, and apprentice programs. They can be extremely valuable options for people who are not interested in attending a 4-year university.

Also, don't forget about alternative high schools. I taught for a while at an alternative high school where students learned a trade and got a GED. They still learned all of the basic academic skills, but they were taught using hands-on or vocation-related activities. For example, we had an automotive program where kids learned how to fix cars. We also had apprentice programs for electricians, carpenters, and plumbers.

These programs were very successful, and students had to work hard to get through them. By the time they graduated, students typically had jobs that paid more than I make.

UNDEREMPLOYMENT

As you can probably imagine, the result of not getting a high school diploma is being unemployed or underemployed. The secondary result is living in poverty.

According to the Learning Disabilities Association of America (2007), 62% of students with learning disabilities are unemployed a year after leaving high school. Of those who do work, most will work part-time and will not receive benefits such as medical insurance.

I hope that you see the importance of this topic. I am not saying that people have to be doctors or lawyers and make a million dollars a year to be successful and happy. However, being gainfully employed certainly has many advantages over being unemployed. In addition to being able to pay for things, such as food and rent, there is the sense of accomplishment, the ability to become friends with your coworkers, and . . . well, just getting out of your house and spending your day doing something.

I am guessing that you agree with me that employment is a worthy goal. The question then becomes, how do you help enhance your child's vocational opportunities? The most important thing is to instill in your child, as early as possible, the expectation that he or she will be a valued and productive member of society. Encourage your child to do something with his or her life.

This, of course, is easier said than done. But there are many easy and practical things that you can do to foster this sense of purpose. For example, encourage young children to play make-believe. Ask them what they want to be when they grow up, and no matter what they say, never tell them that something is unrealistic. Even if they want to be a rock star or an actor, encourage them to dream and to work toward their goals. Maybe they will even be the next—heaven forbid—Britney Spears. And if they don't make the big time, they may find their real calling along the way. For example, rather than become a world-famous rock star, maybe your child will fall in love with teaching music. Maybe your child will turn out like the main character from the movie *Mr. Holland's Opus*.

The point here is that your child has to believe that he can do something with his life. Yes, he also needs the skills, such as the ability to study and learn, as I mentioned earlier. But without the motivation to take risks and apply for jobs and to try new things, your child's vocational life will be rather limited.

MEMORY

Another key characteristic of individuals who have learning disabilities involves memory. Specifically, as I talk about in chapter 1, they tend to have problems processing information so that it can be stored and retrieved effectively.

This is a huge problem. Think about it. Think about all of the aspects of your life that would be affected if you had difficulty recalling pertinent information right when you needed it. For example, imagine how well you would do in a job interview or on a date if you kept forgetting someone's name or information that was just given to you. You probably wouldn't get the job or another opportunity to go out with the person. Imagine how slowly you would learn new tasks if you had to struggle to recall prerequisite knowledge. As your teacher is explaining how to do algebra, you are constantly trying to remember your multiplication facts. And so on.

So, what can we do about this poor memory? Well, before we can do anything, we have to understand what memory is and why your child may have a poor one. According to most theorists, you have several kinds of memory: short-term memory, working memory, and long-term memory. But there are other factors that come into play, such as attention, storage, and retrieval. All of these work together in what we call *memory*. Maybe an example will help.

Right now, you are looking at this page. Your eyes are sensing the letters written in black ink on a more or less white piece of paper, and they are sending the information to your brain through the neuropathways that I discussed a couple of chapters back. Your brain has to process the information and make sense of it. After all, your eyes aren't just sensing the letters. They are also sensing a billion other things—the shadow down the middle of the book, a small hair from your cat that somehow got stuck on the page, maybe a little stain from last night's ravioli, and so forth. Plus, your skin, ears, nose, and mouth are also bombarding your brain with what they are sensing. Your brain has a great deal going on.

Most of the data that your senses are sending to your brain are dismissed. For example, your fingertips are feeling this book, but you were probably not very aware of it until just now. The same is true with regard to your sensing that you are wearing socks and underwear or are listening to the passing of cars by your window. Most of these stimuli are filtered out. You aren't paying attention to them.

The stimuli that you are paying attention to need to be reworked and organized into something meaningful. Keep in mind that what your eyes are seeing are actually black symbols on a white page. Your brain needs to translate these symbols into something meaningful to effectively remember it. This takes place while information is in the working memory, which involves what you are thinking at this very moment. It is like the desktop on your computer. Whatever you are working on must be on your computer's desktop.

Working memory is a subset of your short-term memory. After you read these words, they disappear from your working memory, and their meanings linger for a while in your short-term memory. So, if I were to have you stop reading at this very moment and summarize what this chapter is about, you probably wouldn't be able to retrieve exactly what the chapter said. But you would be able to recall from your short-term memory the gist of what I have discussed.

If I keep examining the same theme over and over again (e.g., that people with learning disabilities aren't stupid and that they can succeed in life), these messages will eventually move from your short-term memory to your long-term memory. This is called *storage*.

We store a bunch of things in our long-term memories, but we might have problems recalling, or *retrieving*, them. For example, you spent an entire year sitting next to someone when you were in third grade. You most likely heard that person's name hundreds of times. In other words, that classmate's name went from your working memory to your short-term memory and then eventually to your long-term memory.

For many years, you knew this person's name. When you were in fourth grade and saw him on the playground, you probably knew instantly who he was because you could retrieve that information from your long-term memory. But do you know his name now? If I showed you a picture of your third-grade classmate, could you recall who he is? Maybe . . . if you thought about it for awhile.

The point is that just because something is transmitted to your long-term memory doesn't mean you have a good memory. You also have to be able to retrieve the data that you want from long-term memory.

Unfortunately, people with learning disabilities tend to have two problems that impair their ability to remember things. First, they have a general difficulty processing stimuli into something meaningful. The specific difficulty depends largely on the types of learning disabilities that they have.

For instance, I have an auditory learning disability. I have a horrible time processing what I hear. When you tell me your name or phone number, I can't always translate the sounds that you make into something that makes sense to me. The same is true for people with dyslexia. They have problems translating what they read into recognizable letters and words. Consequently, many things that I am told and many things that dyslexics read never end up in our long-term memories.

Second, people with learning disabilities often have problems recalling what they need to recall from their long-term memories. For instance, let's suppose that I really like you and want to remember your name. So I expel tremendous energy forcing myself to pay attention to what you say your name is. I keep repeating your name in my head, making it go from working memory to short-term memory to long-term memory. However, when I see you again, I can't recall your name. Maybe I know that it starts with a *J* or maybe it is on the tip of my tongue, but I can't fully retrieve it.

What can you do to help your child improve her memory? It depends largely on the disability that she has. If she has difficulty processing information so that it goes into her long-term memory, she can try saying the information out loud, writing it down several times, or utilizing the information in different ways.

Alternately, if he has difficulty retrieving information from long-term memory, he will need to learn how to organize what he has learned. One way to do so is to create *associations*. For instance, when I was in college, I met this girl whom I really liked. I wanted to remember her name, so I identified the most striking thing about her (her red hair) and tied it to her name (Rebecca). I kept thinking *redhead Rebecca, redhead Rebecca*. When I saw her again, seeing her red hair automatically triggered her name.

I talk about additional strategies when I address specific types of learning disabilities in later chapters. But I hope that you get the idea.

SUMMARY

People with learning disabilities are diverse. Get a hundred people with learning disabilities together, and you will likely have many types of learners. However, several characteristics are common across all learning disabilities. For example, people with learning disabilities tend to have poor self-esteem. They tend to be unemployed or underemployed. They are often afraid to take risks.

When trying to help children, you can't focus on only the academic problems they are having. For instance, if your child has dyslexia, you can't merely address reading. You have to also help with all of the other things that go along with having a learning disability, such as the issues discussed in this chapter.

5

DYSLEXIA: LEARNING
DISABILITIES OF READING

The first specific learning disability that I want to discuss involves reading. Why start here? Well, to begin with, reading learning disabilities are probably the most prominent—though not the most common, mind you. Many people have learning disabilities in nonreading areas, such as writing. It is just that dyslexia seems to stand out the most.

Why is it so noticeable? Well, if people have a learning disability in, say, receptive language, how would you know? Or expressive language? Or math? Unless you really quizzed them about what they heard, or had them speak a lot or do math problems, you probably wouldn't discover their difficulties. Reading disabilities, however, are pretty far-reaching. They affect one's ability to get information out of a newspaper, order off of a menu, follow the rules of the road, fill out a job application, and many, many other activities. Moreover, reading is one of those areas that is tested early and often in the public schools. Kids as young as 4 years old are assessed to see if they know their ABCs. They read aloud in class. And so forth.

Another reason why I want to start off with reading disabilities is that they are probably the most devastating to a person's academic development. Now, before you start thinking that other disabilities are less important than reading learning disabilities, please let me explain.

As I said before, reading is a pretty integral part of life. If you have trouble reading, your life is going to be affected on many fronts, many more than if you have problems in math or writing. For instance, being poor in math wouldn't necessarily prevent you from becoming a social studies teacher or a writer. However, not being able to read will certainly affect your ability to learn an array of subjects and thus impair your ability to earn the education and abilities needed to become what you like.

So, that is why I want to talk about reading learning disabilities first. If your child doesn't have any problems with reading, then I suggest that you skip this chapter—unless you are just interested in this topic. We'll catch up to you in a little bit.

WHAT IS DYSLEXIA?

If you are like most people, you have probably heard of the term *dyslexia*. You might even know someone with dyslexia. So, the question arises, what is it?

The short answer is that *dyslexia* is a general term for a type or group of learning disabilities. It is often referred to as *letter blindness*, and it primarily affects a person's ability to read. For example, letters may move around and be blurry. However, there is far more to dyslexia that just this. But before I get into the various other characteristics of people with dyslexia, I want to first talk about what reading is.

So, what is reading? This sounds like an odd question, but before I can talk about problems in reading, you have to understand what reading is.

Reading is a process by which we give meaning to written symbols. It involves two steps: decoding and comprehension. Decoding is the manner by which we perceive the written symbols and turn them into something that we recognize. Several factors can affect how well you decode written information. For example, to decode written material, you have to be able to actually see the letters (or, in the case of Braille users, feel the letters), so visual acuity can be an issue. That is why students who have vision impairments often have problems reading as well. In addition to visual acuity, the ability of your eyes to track the page in unison can affect decoding. If the muscles in your eyes do not have uniformed strength and control, your eyes will not work together as they scan across these lines. In such cases, your vision might be blurred or distorted. Comprehension is the ability to make sense out of the letters and symbols that the eyes see. It isn't just about having the proper vocabulary. It involves how the brain recalls words. Perhaps, I should explain.

Remember back in the second chapter when we talked about the brain and the causes of learning disabilities? We discussed how learning disabilities were most likely caused by abnormalities in certain areas of the brain. These abnormalities make it difficult for people with learning disabilities to process certain information effectively.

Well, in the case of a learning disability in reading, the areas of the brain that control visual recognition of written language are most likely affected. When someone with this type of learning disability sees letters on a page, his or her brain has to work extra hard to figure out what the letters are and what words they are forming. Moreover, in addition to having difficulty figuring out what words the letters are forming, people with learning disabilities may also have difficulty figuring out what a word means. Again, this isn't attributed to a lack of vocabulary or a low IQ. It is just that when people see the letters *c-a-t*, the part of the brain that *translates* the word, or gives it meaning, struggles a bit.

Maybe I can illustrate this a bit better. Remember when we talked about associative and cognitive thinking? Associative thinking is when you can do things without really focusing on them. The example that I used involved your being able to drive to work without having to focus too much on what you are doing. You don't have to actively think about where to turn or how far you have to push down the accelerator. If you have been driving for many years, you do everything naturally, as if you were on automatic pilot. Cognitive thinking is where you have to focus on what you are doing, much like when you drive a car for the first time. You have to focus on which way to turn the wheel, how forcefully to step on the breaks, and when to put the turn signal on.

For you and me and other people without dyslexia, reading is an associative process. We can look at most of these words and make sense out of them. For example, you can look at words like *the, and, of, for*, and so forth, and simply know them. You don't have to break them down or sound them out. You see *t-h-e* and your brain thinks *the*.

For people with dyslexia, reading is a cognitive process. They are much like people who are learning a new language. They have to work a little harder to decode and comprehend what they see. They have to process each part of the word to make sense of the whole. They come across words like *the*, *and*, *of*, and so forth, and they have to give them meaning, which takes time and energy.

The main idea here is that people with learning disabilities in reading don't have a vision problem. There is nothing wrong with their eyes. They have a processing problem. They have difficulty processing what they see into meaningful information.

Now that we have some understanding about what reading is, let's look at what having a learning disability in reading means. But before I begin, I want to point out that because you have problems reading doesn't mean that you have a learning disability. There are literally hundreds of other explanations. For instance, you might have problems with reading because you have poor vision and can't see this page clearly. You might not be able to read because the writing is in a language that you don't know. Or the words that the author uses might be over your head. Or—dread the thought—the author might actually write so poorly that you can't keep your attention focused long enough to understand the main point!

You might also have problems concentrating because of environmental distractions or conditions such as ADHD or petite mal seizures. Or you could have mental retardation and simply have difficulty learning new things. Or you were never exposed to reading when you were little. Or maybe you just hate reading and aren't really trying. The list goes on and on.

The point is that your child might be having difficulty reading for many, many reasons. Furthermore, none of the reasons that I mention are actually the result of a specific learning disability. To have a reading learning disability, your child has to have problems reading but for an unknown reason. In other words, she can't read as well as she should, and the reason why is not attributed her eyesight, vocabulary, intelligence, the quality of the writing, an environmental distraction, a lack of trying, or anything like that.

So, before any diagnosis of a learning disability is made, you should help rule out some of the other possibilities. Make sure that your child has a thorough eye exam. Compare his reading ability to his spoken vocabulary. Is there a huge difference? Is your child behind in all other subjects? If so, then it probably isn't a learning disability in reading causing the problem.

CHARACTERISTICS OF INDIVIDUALS WITH LEARNING DISABILITIES IN READING

As with people with learning disabilities in general, individuals with learning disabilities in reading are a diverse group. They can experience any one (and more than one) of the following difficulties.

Inconsistency

First of all, many people with learning disabilities in reading can read. They might actually read very well, at least at times. At other times, unfortunately, they can't read at all, or their reading is significantly impaired. In other words, their reading is inconsistent.

This often confuses teachers and parents. They know that a child can read. They have seen the child do it before. So when a child mispronounces words, struggles, or simply can't read, the parents and teachers believe that the child isn't trying or is just "acting silly." The parents and teachers then try to motivate the child through rewards or punishment, but neither will work. In the end, everyone just gets frustrated.

Reversals

One of the stereotypic problems that kids with learning disabilities in reading have is reversing their letters. For example, they might look at a b and see a q, p, or d. Moreover, they might look at an E or an L, and their brains may tell them that it is a 3 or a 7. Basically, for whatever reason, their brains get things all twisted around.

Swirling

Sometimes, people with learning disabilities in reading actually see the words move around the page. As the readers are looking at these words and letters, they appear to twist or swirl around the center of the page. One of my students used to say that the words on the page would "dance" around in a circle.

Rivers

In addition to seeing words swirl or dance, students with reading learning disabilities might also see rivers of white space streaming down the page. The rivers would appear to move, which, as you can imagine, makes it extremely difficult to concentrate. Just try to read the passage in Figure 5.1, from J. R. R. Tolkien's *The Hobbit*. Notice how the spaces between the words seem to form rivers that trickle down the passage?

Sliding

Another common movement issue is that words from one line suddenly appear in another. So, let's say that you are trying to read the following two sentences, which appear one on top of the other:

It was a dark and stormy night.
Suddenly, a gunshot sounded.

However, as you are trying to read, the words shift around. You end up reading the sentence "Suddenly, it was a gunshot sounded." Needless to say, you would probably be confused and would have to read the sentences over again.

A variation of this problem is that students will read a line of text and then come back to the beginning of the line rather than drop down to the next one. So in the example, you might read, "It was a dark and stormy night. It was a dark and stormy night . . . " And so on.

Inahole   intheground   thereliveda   hobbit.
Notanasty,   dirty,wet   hole,filled   with the ends
of   wormsand   an oozy smell,   nor
yetadry,   bare,sandy   hole with   nothing
in ittosit   downonoreat:it   wasa   hobbit   -hole,
andthat means   comfort.

Figure 5.1.   Rivers of White Space Within a Passage of *The Hobbit*

Dysfluency

Consider this for a second. You have problems reading. Letters appear backward, words move around the page, or whatever. You are sitting in class, and the teacher asks you to read a passage out loud. How well are you going to perform? Probably, not very well.

Even when kids with learning disabilities in reading don't see words or letters moving around, reading out loud can be quite problematic. The kids often sound like robots, saying each word after a halting pause. However, just because a child doesn't read well out loud doesn't mean that she has a reading problem. After all, she could have a speaking problem. Maybe she stutters or gets nervous when speaking in public, or she has something called *dysnomia*—an expressive language learning disability (which I discuss later).

Comprehension

In addition to having all kinds of visual problems, many students with learning disabilities in reading also have problems with comprehension. As I said in an earlier section, these difficulties are not the result of poor vocabulary. They are caused by the individual's inability to process the words quickly. While you are zooming through these words, putting meaning to each word as soon as you decode it, individuals with learning disabilities have to think about what the words are conveying.

For instance, suppose that we go back to the earlier example and you read, "It was a dark and stormy night." Even if you don't see the letters reverse, swirl around, or make rivers of blank spaces, you may still have difficulty understanding what you read. It is as if you have to think about each word. Thus, you would probably have to say to yourself,

"It was" . . . that means the situation is in the past tense. So it isn't happening now. It is happened a while ago. "Dark" means black or hard to see. "Stormy" means that there was rain and probably a lot of wind. "Night" means that it isn't day. So, in other words, what I am reading means that it was a night that was really raining and blowing and it was hard to see.

Can you appreciate how long and tiresome it would be to have a reading disability? Not only would you have problems seeing the words, but

even if you saw things perfectly clear, you might have a tough time figuring out what everything meant.

WAYS TO HELP INDIVIDUALS WITH
READING LEARNING DISABILITIES

Do any of the characteristics discussed here sound familiar? If they do,
you are probably wondering what you can do to help your child learn
how to read. Fortunately, there are many strategies that you can use.

But before you can select a strategy to help your child, you need to
first understand what problems he or she is having and why. For example, if comprehension is a problem, you need to utilize strategies that
build comprehension. If the letters are moving around, you need to try
one of the other strategies. If you don't know exactly what characteristics your child displays, ask the person who evaluated him or her. Better
yet, ask your child. Simply talking to your child might help you understand a great deal about what is going on.

Red and Green Transparencies

Have you ever seen a 3-D movie? You know, where you had to wear
those funny cardboard glasses? One lens was made of red plastic, the
other of green plastic. The glasses were what made the movie look as if
it were jumping out at you.

Studies have found that many people with reading learning disabilities are able to read better with such glasses. Apparently, the glasses
help stop letters from moving around and reversing. It sounds strange,
but there is some logic behind it. You see, as you are looking at this page,
light is reflecting off of the white paper and into your eyes. Light doesn't
reflect off of the black letters. Technically speaking, your eyes really
don't see the letters. What they "see" is an absence of light from where
the letters are. In other words, as you are looking at this page, your eyes
are seeing a white page and a bunch of blank spots. Your brain then
translates the blank spots into letters.

Some researchers believe that people who see letters moving and reversing do so because their brains get overwhelmed by all of the white

spaces and thus have difficulty translating the blank spaces into something meaningful. If you invert the colors of the print and paper (i.e., print white letters on a black page), the reverses and movement should diminish.

But printing white on black is rather difficult. First of all, you need to find black paper. Then you have to find pens that write in white ink. This isn't exactly an easy task. Instead, you can put red or green transparencies over a normal page. Transparencies are also called *overheads*. Teachers write on them and then project what they wrote onto a screen in front of the class. They can be found in any office supply store.

If you put red or green transparencies over normal text, such as that in this book, the black letters seem to stand out more. They become bolder and easier to read. The white part of the page also doesn't overwhelm the brain as much as it did before.

Viewfinder

If your child has a tendency to see words and letters jump from one line to the next, there is a simple solution: Use what is often referred to as a *viewfinder*.

A viewfinder is a devise though which a reader can see the line that is being read, but nothing else. Basically, it is a piece of paper or cardboard that has a little slit as long as the book's page and as wide as the book's print. They are very easy to make.

The idea is that the viewfinder prevents the reader from being distracted by all of the other words above and below the line that is being read. One of my current students swears by it. She even put a piece of red plastic, such as that from the transparencies just discussed, over the slit. She keeps one in her backpack and uses it whenever I have her read something in class.

Knowing When to Read

Perhaps, the most important strategy for children with learning disabilities involves knowing when to read. You see, as I mention earlier in this chapter, people with learning disabilities don't have problems all of the time. Sometimes, my students can read fine. Other times, it is a tremendous struggle. The trick is knowing when the best time to read is.

From my experience, it seems that students intuitively know when the good and bad times are. Just ask them. They will probably be able to tell you. If they don't know offhand, conduct some tests. Have your child read at various times of the day, and keep a chart of his or her progress. You will probably find that certain times of the day are better than others. For instance, most of my students who have reading learning disabilities say that they are able to read and comprehend better in the morning. As the day goes along, they claim, their eyes get tired and the reversals and movement begin.

If your child reads better at certain times, have him or her do most of the reading then. This isn't rocket science or anything. You just have to ask the correct questions and keep your eyes open. Then figure out how to best help your child.

Environmental Distracters

In addition to asking your child about when he or she reads best, also ask where he or she learns best. You might be surprised what you find. For example, there have been studies that have found that rooms with florescent lights are horrible for kids with learning disabilities. The lights are harsh and vibrate. I myself get headaches when I am around florescent lights too long.

Unfortunately, most classrooms seem to use nothing but florescent lights. So, I frequently suggest that teachers soften them. There are a couple of ways to do this. One is to drape colored tissue paper so that it filters the light a little. However, be careful not to let the tissue paper to get too close to the bulb. You don't want to start a fire!

Another strategy is to simply turn off the overhead lights and bring in floor lamps. If you do so, I strongly recommend that you use full-spectrum bulbs. They are less harsh than florescent bulbs, and studies have found that they help people with depression and ADHD.

Other environmental distracters often involve noise. Surprisingly, many of my students, as well as I, cannot read when it is too quiet. Every little creak and groan of the world becomes distracting. Even the ticking of the clock in our classroom drives us crazy. So, I tend to use background music or white noise. Right now I am listening to a soft jazz CD. It calms me down and allows me to focus. It also drowns out all of the noises that tend to distract me.

The bottom line is this: Don't just assume that your child is having problems reading because of a learning disability. Maybe there is something in the environment that is distracting your child. And even if your child does have a learning disability, minimizing environmental distractions should be your first step in helping him or her learn.

Read in Brief Spurts

Yet another practical commonsense strategy for dealing with dyslexia is to limit reading to short periods of time. Again, the idea is that most mistakes tend to be made when the student is anxious or fatigued.

How much is too much reading? That is difficult to say. A colleague of mine uses a program of "5 minutes on, 5 minutes off." She has her students read for 5 minutes and then discuss what they read for 5 minutes. They then go back and read for 5 more minutes and so forth. Not only do the 5-minute discussions help her students process the information, but they also give the students' eyes a rest.

Use Context Clues

Helping your child read words is one thing. Helping him or her understand what he or she has read is another. Students, of course, need to do both.

One way to promote comprehension is to discuss the material with children right after they have finished reading it or during the reading process, such as in the 5-minute program previously discussed. Another way is to teach children how to utilize context clues as they read.

Context clues are anything that can give the reader hints as to what the material is about. For example, let's suppose that your child is reading a book and there is a picture of a giant on the cover. Well, that is a good indication that there will be a giant in the story. So when your child comes to a word that starts with a *g* and ends in *ant*, she can guess *giant*.

Another example of context clues lies in using words in a sentence to help determine the meaning of a word or the passage. For example, suppose that you read the sentence "Bill threw the balgbil to Susie, who tagged Ricky out." You probably don't know what a *balgbil* is. As a matter of fact, I know that you don't. I just made it up. But I bet you can guess what I meant, given what the sentence is about. A *balgbil* is a big ball.

Direct Instruction

If you have been around special educators for long, you have undoubtedly heard of the term *direct instruction*, which means different things to different people. Basically speaking, it is a systematic way of teaching students information, especially, reading and basic mathematics. Direct instruction is highly structured and often scripted. It provides extensive repetitious practice and immediate feedback.

An example of direct instruction as it applies to reading might involve having the teacher stand in front of the class and point to a letter on the board. "This is an *A*," the teacher would say and then ask, "What is it?" In unison, the class would reply, "A."

After providing immediate feedback, such as saying "Good!" the teacher goes on to the next letter. She keeps going through the alphabet over and over again until the students have mastered it.

Direct instruction has also been dubbed "drill and kill" by critics who claim that it teaches only memorization and not higher thinking, such as comprehension or analytical skills. However, there is considerable research indicating that direct instruction can be quite useful in teaching students rudimentary skills.

Phonics

Another highly contentious debate in special education involves the use of phonics versus the whole language approach to teaching reading. Depending on what side you listen to, one strategy is wonderful, the other horrid. Personally, I have seen both strategies work extremely well, and I have seen both strategies fail miserably. I suggest that you try both and see which works best for your students.

There are many types of phonic programs. However, in general, phonics emphasizes teaching children, often though direct instruction, the sounds that each letter makes and each letter combination makes.

Students then learn how to read by being able to pronounce whatever word they come across.

Whole Language

Whole language is a strategy for teaching reading that emphasizes all language arts at the same time. For instance, it teaches comprehension, spelling, writing, and reading. Teachers who teach reading via whole language might give a child a story with lots of pictures and then have the child guess what the story is about. The child doesn't have to read each word of the story to be successful. He just has to generate a rough idea about the story's meaning.

Prereading

When you were a student, what was the first thing that you did when you had a reading assignment? You probably looked at the first word and then the second and then the third and so forth until you finished the entire assignment. Right? Well, don't do that!

The first thing that you should do when you have a reading assignment is preread. Basically, what this entails is looking over the passage for clues regarding what is important. For example, you should look at the title of the passage. If it says "Reading Learning Disabilities," then that gives you a good idea what the subject will be. This also gives you a clue about what is important to pay attention to and remember. You should do the same thing with headers of sections, as well as captions under pictures and graphs.

Next, you should read the study guide questions at the beginning of the chapter (if there are any) and then the conclusion—yes, the conclusion. The conclusion gives readers a nice concise summary about all of the main points made in the chapter. Often, you can read the summary and understand the material so well that you don't need to read the chapter itself. This isn't cheating. It is simply effective studying.

Active Reading

For many parents and teachers, teaching reading comprehension is a matter of memorizing vocabulary words. And although that might work for some students, there are many students who simply cannot retain information that they have read even though they know all of the words. For instance, you might understand each and every word that I have used on this page. However, you might not be able to remember what this chapter is about seconds after you set the book down. So what do you do? You need to read actively, which is what you need to teach your child to do when confronted with reading assignments.

To teach your child how to read actively, instruct her to not just sit there and say each word in her head (passive reading) but rather read a paragraph or a page and then summarize, in her own words, what she just read. Also encourage your child to ask herself questions. For example, have her stop and ask herself, "What is the author trying to tell me?" "What is the main point here?" "What is important for me to remember?" "Is there a reoccurring theme or topic?" And so on.

You can also have your child guess at what she thinks is going to happen next. In other words, teach your child to get involved with what is being read. Don't just emphasize how to say each word correctly. Talk about what the words mean and how they are telling the reader something important.

Reading Recovery

Reading Recovery is a popular program that teaches young children how to read. It involves a one-on-one tutor and intensive reading instruction that is geared toward the needs of the individual child. It has been found to be quite effective. For more information or for Reading Recovery programs in your area, go to www.readingrecovery.org.

Appropriate Reading Material

One of the main problems that teachers and parents have when working with students who have learning disabilities involves motivating them to read. I am sure that it often seems like an uphill battle. But it doesn't have to be. If you can find some reading material that actually interests your child, you are well on your way to helping him become a better reader.

The reading material can be anything—magazines, newspapers, even comic books. Any reading is good reading. So figure out what interests your child and then get reading material about those topics.

SUMMARY

The first specific learning disability discussed thus far is often referred to as *dyslexia*, which is a term typically used to describe any learning disability that adversely affects reading.

As with those who have learning disabilities in general, dyslexics are a diverse population. Some dyslexics have difficulty reading only from time to time; as a result, their reading abilities appear inconsistent. Other dyslexics see letters moving around so frequently that they have difficulty reading nearly all of the time.

In addition to seeing letters and words move or distort, individuals with learning disabilities in reading might also have difficulty comprehending what they read. The reason is not that they lack the vocabulary or have low IQs. It is just one of the many characteristics of their condition.

In this chapter, I talk about what a learning disability in reading is like. I also discuss several strategies that might help your child. The next topic that I cover is dysgraphia, which is a learning disability that affects writing. It is often confused with dyslexia, so you might want to at least glance through the following chapter.

6

DYSGRAPHIA: LEARNING
DISABILITIES OF WRITING

The next type of learning disability that I want to discuss involves writing. There is no particular reason why this is our second stop on our tour of specific learning disabilities. I am not putting these conditions in any kind of order (e.g., from most to least prevalent or from most to least severe). The topic of writing just seems to flow well after our discussion about reading. After all, many people who have problems with reading will have problems with writing. For instance, a dyslexic who sees letters moving around and reversing will undoubtedly copy what she sees. We'll talk more about this in a moment.

Additionally, talking about reading and writing makes sense because of their relationship. As students learn to read, they also learn how to write. And so here we are.

Unlike reading, little is known about specific learning disabilities that involve writing. There is something called *dysgraphia*, which I explore in a moment, but it is poorly defined and not understood well. Furthermore, it is rarely used as a diagnosis, not because it is rare, but because few people seem to know about it.

As with reading, not everyone who has trouble writing has a learning disability. There are tons of other explanations for difficulty with writing. For example, perhaps you have issues with fine motor skills, much like someone with cerebral palsy, and you can't hold your pencil or move it properly. Or perhaps you have vision problems and can't see what you are writing. Or maybe English is not your native language and you have difficulty finding the correct word and how to spell it. Or perhaps you have an attention disorder and simply can't focus on what you are doing and you make careless mistakes. Or perhaps you are hyperactive and you rush when you write, thus making your handwriting sloppy. The list goes on and on.

In other words, it is really important that all other possibilities be ruled out before a diagnosis is made. This is important for all learning disabilities but especially for matters involving writing and similar fine motor skills. If your child is clumsy, physically weak, or uncoordinated, bring him to a doctor. Why? Because it could be something serious.

A student in a neighboring school district was having a lot of problems with hand–eye coordination. His handwriting was horrid. He fumbled around, often dropping things. He fell down a lot and so forth. For a while, the school thought that he might be drinking, but he didn't have any other signs of intoxication. He didn't slur his speech, seem inhibited, or anything of the sort. Eventually, his parents brought him to a doctor, and after a series of tests, the boy was diagnosed with a brain tumor. Thankfully, he is fine now.

I am not trying to scare you. I am just trying to make the point that learning disabilities can often mimic other, potentially life-threatening conditions. Before being diagnosed with any learning disability, your child should have a comprehensive examination that can rule out some of the other possibilities.

Okay, enough scary stuff. Let's get back to learning disabilities that affect writing.

You might be sitting there thinking, "What's the big deal? I have really sloppy handwriting, too. It doesn't affect my life at all."

And you are probably correct. However, as I am about to discuss, learning disabilities in writing don't just affect handwriting. They affect other aspects of life as well.

WHAT IS DYSGRAPHIA?

If you haven't heard of the term *dysgraphia*, you aren't alone. Few teachers have either. Loosely translated, *dysgraphia* means a problem with writing. However, as I talk about in the introduction to this chapter, it affects far more than just writing, but we'll get to that in a second.

Many people with dysgraphia are misdiagnosed with dyslexia because both learning disabilities are characterized by poor handwriting and writing letters backward. But the underlying cause is completely different. The dyslexic looks at a letter, such as b, and sees it as a p, d, or q. So that is what he writes. In other words, he writes what he sees.

The dysgraphic sees things perfectly fine. If you show her a b, she sees a b. However, she has difficulty with her hand–eye coordination. After she makes the downward vertical line of the b, she accidentally makes the loop to the left rather than to the right, thus making a d. Do you see the difference between the two conditions?

They both write the wrong letter, d for b. But a dyslexic can have neat handwriting and simply write what he sees, which is wrong. A dysgraphic can have sloppy handwriting and see letters fine, but she writes them incorrectly.

Another major difference is that dyslexics, by definition, have difficulties reading. Dysgraphics should read fine. Again, it is their hand–eye coordination that makes their writing problematic. Perhaps, I can explain what dysgraphia is a bit better.

If you were to close your eyes, you would probably be able to write your name or whatever you wanted without looking down. Kids with dysgraphia have a hard time doing this. They may be able to picture the letters that they want to write, but their hands have difficulty reproducing them, especially when they aren't concentrating.

Remember associative versus cognitive thinking in the first chapter? That applies here as well. You see, when you write your name, it is an associative process. You can do it without thinking. As a matter of fact, I bet you can write your name while talking to someone and tap dancing, all at the same time.

For dysgraphics, writing is a cognitive process. They have to focus their attention on what they are doing. They have to consciously think to themselves, "Okay, I want to write my name. The first letter is R. First, I have to make an upward vertical line. Then I have to make a loop that goes to the right. Right is that way . . . " Can you imagine how frustrating it would be to write something? Can you appreciate how long it would take to write your homework if you had to think this deeply about each and every letter?

Want to experience having dysgraphia? Bring this book into your bathroom. Hold up the picture of the maze in Figure 6.1 so that it is facing away from you and reflecting into the mirror. Now, with your finger or a pencil, try to trace your way through the maze using only its reflection; that is, do not look down at the actual page. It's kind of tough, isn't it? In many ways, this is how a person with dysgraphia feels when writing.

Your lines will probably be all messy, especially the ones that you wanted to make straight. Furthermore, you will probably have to double back and loop around because your hand went the wrong direction. I hope that this helps you understand what it is like having dysgraphia as far as the hand–eye coordination goes.

But this disorientation isn't just spatial. It also involves sequences, such as following directions in order, spelling correctly, and writing thoughts sequentially. As you will see, dysgraphia can significantly affect many aspects of a child's academic life.

Figure 6.1. Hold this image of a maze up to a mirror and try to work your way through it without looking down at the actual page—that is, use the image in the mirror. Feeling like a dysgraphic? *Source:* Clickmazes (2000)

CHARACTERISTICS OF INDIVIDUALS WITH LEARNING DISABILITIES IN WRITING

Let's go into more detail about the characteristics of individuals with dysgraphia. Maybe you will see some of them in your child.

Handwriting

Perhaps, the most obvious characteristic of individuals with learning disabilities in writing is poor handwriting. People with learning disabilities in writing often have problems with spacing. That is, they tend to write letters too close to each other so that the letters are nearly right on top of each other, or they space out letters so that each letter appears as a separate word.

Another problem with handwriting involves proportions. For example, some letters appear much too big whereas others are tiny and difficult to read. Capital letters might even be smaller than lowercase letters, which is problematic given that the size of many letters helps distinguish them from others. For example, an *l* that isn't tall enough will look like an undotted *i*.

Last, individuals with learning disabilities in writing often have poor handwriting. Even if they use perfect spacing and appropriate proportions, what they write is illegible. *O*'s can be skinny or flat so that they look like undotted *i*'s or even *e*'s.

Spelling

Another common characteristic of people with dysgraphia in writing is poor spelling. Like with children with dyslexia, dysgraphics may reverse letters, such as writing *taecher* for *teacher* or *wrold* for *world*. They might also get letters completely out of sequence, making it looked as if they wrote random letters. For instance, they might spell *water* as *tware* or *education* as *auctioned*.

More likely, however, they will probably spell words phonetically, that is, by how they sound. For example, they might write *mast* for *must*, *lit* for *light*, *tip* for *type*, or *mak* for *make*. The problem isn't that they are stupid, that the letters are moving around, or that they don't know how to spell certain words. It is that they tend to get the order of them all confused. It is as if they have the letters floating around in their heads but grab them out of sequence without even knowing it.

Additionally, the English language has a great many irregularities. For instance, consider the ending *-ough*. You would think that those letters put together would produce the same sound all of the time, but they don't. Say *cough*. Now say *through*. Now say *though*. Do you hear all of the differences? It is very confusing.

Plus, there are all of these rules to remember, and then there are the contradictions to the rules. For example, an popular one is *i* before *e* except after *c* (and sometimes *w*). But there are many, many more. No wonder spelling is so difficult for some people!

Written Expression

Perhaps, the most detrimental problem that kids with dysgraphia have involves their ability to express themselves in writing. I am not referring back to what I have already talked about—poor handwriting and spelling. Kids with dysgraphia have difficulty putting their thoughts into words.

It isn't that they have writer's block or don't know what to write. Nor is it that they don't have the vocabulary to say what they want to say. Those aren't the problems at all. The problem is that they tend to have significant difficulty following the rules of writing, such as creating sentences with correct structure. In fact, one of my college students who has dysgraphia cannot seem to put the words that she wants to say in proper order. Here is an e-mail that she sent to me a couple of weeks ago (misspellings included):

> Dtr Cimera,
>   Will I not be in clas next class. Me and my family am going for Chsrt-mas Break early to Florida seeing my sister and their new baby Justin that we haven't seen yet for the first time which I am really looking frowad to!! Thanks for understanding. Have a good break.

Believe it or not, this is a real e-mail! Let's use it as a way to illustrate issues related to written expression.

Now, I am sure that you can get the ideas that my student was trying to convey. She won't be in class the next time we meet because she is going to Florida, where she is going to see her sister and her new nephew, Justin, whom she hasn't seen before. But her writing is horrendous. When she writes, the words tend to be out of their proper order. Instead of writing *I will not be in class*, she put the *will* first, making it sound as if she were asking a question. Furthermore, she (like most kids with dysgraphia) has poor word choice. Although there is nothing technically wrong with using the same word twice in one sentence, writing *I will not be in class next class* doesn't flow as well as *I will not be in class next week*. Finally, her grammar needs a great deal of work. Just take a look at the second sentence. I don't even know where to begin! First of all, it should be *My family and I* not *Me and my family*. Second, it is a run-on sentence. It just keeps going on and on. Third, it keeps switching verb tenses. Ugh. At any rate, I am sure that you see my point.

It is interesting to me that this student doesn't speak this way. Actually, she speaks very well. As she explains it, when she tries to write, it is like she is thinking of four or five things to say and they all get "jumbled up."

So, what do you do to help students like this? How do you teach them to express themselves correctly with legible handwriting and correct spelling? Good questions! I talk about this in a little bit.

Spatial Orientation

In addition to having difficulty writing neatly and coherently, individuals with dysgraphia have problems with spatial orientation. They are likely to get lost, turned around, or easily disoriented. For example, they might think that they are heading toward the exit of the mall when really they are heading in the opposite direction. They also might get their lefts and rights mixed up. I have a story that illustrates this point.

My wife must have a mild form of dysgraphia. Whenever we are in the car and she is giving me directions as I am driving, we inevitably come to an intersection where I have to ask, "Which way?" Without hesitation, she will point right and say "left."

Sometimes, I don't see her pointing, so I naturally go the way she says. As soon I begin turning the car, she starts saying, "What are you doing? Go left. Left!" When I tell her that I am going left, she responds, "Not your left, *my* left," which, of course, is the same thing. And so it goes.

WAYS TO HELP PEOPLE WITH
WRITING LEARNING DISABILITIES

Let's take some time to talk about how you can help your child with a learning disability in written language. The strategies available depend largely on the problems that your child is having. Clearly, if handwriting isn't an issue, then some of what I discuss won't apply to your situation.

Whole Language

In the previous chapter, I talk about whole language in a discussion of reading. Because it applies to written expression, it warrants further comment here.

Basically, whole language is an approach to teaching all of the language arts at the same time. Rather than teach word recognition, comprehension, and spelling and writing in a sequence, all of these subjects are taught at the same time. For example, a child might be asked to write a story, extending a book she just read, using specific spelling and vocabulary words. Rote memorization of spelling and grammar might not be emphasized as much as the enjoyment of written communication and creativity.

This approach is based on the immersion principle. Basically, all activities revolve around the promotion of various language skills.

Direct Instruction

In the previous chapter, I also talk about direct instruction as a way to teach reading, but the same approach can be used to teach spelling. Direct instruction is a teacher-driven strategy that gives students frequent exposure to lessons and immediate feedback. For example, when using direct instruction, a teacher stands in front of the class, shows a flash card with the word *cat* on it, and then says something like "Okay, class, this says 'cat'—*c* . . . *a* . . . *t*. How is it spelled?"

The class then chants in unison as the teacher points to each letter: "*C . . . a . . . t*. Cat."

The teacher keeps going over the words providing positive reinforcement each time the class gets it correct.

Direct instruction can also be used to teach handwriting. For instance, the teacher demonstrates how to write a letter and then has the students model the behavior, making sure that *t*'s are crossed, the *i*'s are dotted, and so forth.

Correct Physical Mechanics of Writing

Many people write sloppy because of their writing implements and how they use them. For example, dull pencils produce lines that are less crisp than those from pencils that have been recently sharpened. Moreover, ballpoint pens that are full of ink will write better than felt pens that leak or are going dry.

But writing implements aren't the only key to good writing. There is also the physical mechanics of writing. For instance, when you write, the only things that should be moving are your thumb and forefinger. Your hand and wrist should be completely stationary. That way, they can stabilize the pencil or pen. If your hand moves, you will have poor control of your writing implement.

Kids also have to be taught how to hold the pen or pencil. Specifically, people should hold it firmly but not tightly. A grip that is too tight produces fatigue and discomfort. Furthermore, the tip of the forefinger should be no closer than three quarters of an inch from the tip of the pencil or pen and no further away than an inch and a quarter.

Why? Well, writing neatly involves having control of the pencil's tip. The closer your fingers are to the tip, the more effort that is needed for you to make large movements. In essence, if you grip the pencil so that it is really close to the tip of your finger, then you have to move your fingers a great deal for your pencil to make the large moments of writing, such as long, continuous up-and-down motion of an *m* or *w*. However, if you grip the pencil too far away, you might lack the control needed to make the smaller movements, such as the loop of an *e* or the subtle swoop of the *j*.

Practice, Practice, Practice

This is going to sound cliché, but most experts agree that developing good handwriting is a matter of practice, not innate ability. After all, there is a lot of hand–eye coordination and muscle memory that one has to develop. You can't just hand children pencils and expect them to print well. Children need time and frequent exposure to learn how to make straight lines, loops, squiggles, and so forth.

Furthermore, frequent practice enable children to become comfortable with writing. The more practice that they receive, the quicker that writing will become second nature. They will no longer have to think about how to write this letter or that. Consequently, their handwriting will become smoother and less herky-jerky.

Checklists and Self-Checking

If you think about it, there are many critical aspects of effective writing, not just the physical aspect of writing, but all of the rules that must be followed to create an exceptional work. For example, capitals have to be larger than lowercase letters. Each sentence has to have a subject, verb, punctuation, and so forth. There is a great deal to remember.

One way that you can help new writers remember everything is to give them a checklist. List all of the things that they tend to forget, such as capitalizing the first letter of the first word of each sentence. That way the student will focus on the act of writing rather than remembering all the rules.

SUMMARY

As I discuss in the first few chapters of this book, there are many types of learning disabilities. In the previous chapter, I investigate learning disabilities in reading, which are often collectively called *dyslexia*. In this chapter, I focus on learning disabilities in writing, which are sometimes referred to as *dysgraphia*.

Dysgraphics have illegible handwriting and may reverse letters. As a result, they might be misdiagnosed as having dyslexia. However, there are at least two distinctions between the two conditions. The first is that dysgraphics write letters backward or inverted because of poor hand–eye coordination. In other words, they see things fine, but when copying, they get all turned around. Dyslexics, however, write things exactly as they see them. Unfortunately, they see words all jumbled up. The second difference between dyslexics and dysgraphics is that dyslexics have problems reading. Again, they see things mixed up. Because dysgraphics see things perfectly, their reading should be unimpaired.

However, poor handwriting and reversals are not the only symptoms of a learning disability in writing. People with dysgraphia may also have problems with spatial orientation and forming grammatically correct sentences. As a result, such disabilities may affect a range of life's activities.

7

DYSCALCULIA: LEARNING DISABILITIES OF MATHEMATICS

The next learning disability that I want to discuss affects mathematics, and it is often called *dyscalculia*. Many people seem to think that this condition is somehow less significant than disabilities in reading or writing. After all, you spend far more of your time reading and writing than doing math. Or do you?

Think of all of the activities that you do on a near-daily basis that require some degree of mathematics. Shopping comes immediately to mind, so does balancing a checkbook. Both of these skills require addition and subtraction. Moreover, they require you to understand the value of money, estimations, and projection of future worth.

There is also cooking. To cook, you have to measure and multiply or divide ingredients according to your taste and the number of people for whom you are cooking. Even basic carpentry and household chores involve some elemental math skills. For example, my wife and I are putting in new baseboards along the edge of our hardwood floors. To figure out how much lumber we needed to buy, we (that is, my wife) had to measure around each wall and then calculate how many boards we required.

And let's not even talk about figuring out our taxes. That involves a lot of math!

In other words, we are surrounded by math problems, whether we realize it or not. In fact, we probably use our math skills just as much as we do our reading and writing skills. At the very least, we regularly use the logic that we get from studying mathematics.

So, what is dyscalculia, and how do you help individuals with it? Great questions! Keep reading.

WHAT IS DYSCALCULIA?

It seems that as soon as I start talking about mathematics, anyone and everyone think that they have a learning disability. However, just because people have problems mastering algebra or trigonometry doesn't mean that they are disabled. After all, not everyone is good at everything.

There is a big difference between people who struggle in math because they don't like it and people who have dyscalculia. Let's revisit an earlier example.

Quick—what is 2 + 2?

I am guessing that you answered right away. "It's 4." And, of course, you are correct.

As I discuss in previous chapters, you probably didn't even have to think about your answer. As soon as you read "What is 2 + 2?" your mind immediately thought "4." It was automatic. Again, the reason is that basic mathematics is an associative process for you.

If you had a learning disability in math (dyscalculia), doing such problems would be a cognitive process. That is, you would have to think about it. You would have to think to yourself,

> Okay. 2 + 2. *Plus* means that it is an addition problem. That means that I am putting two numbers together. What are the two numbers? 2 and 2 . . . and 2 is 1 bigger than 1. Got it. So if I have one 2 and I were to add another 2, I would have . . . 1 . . . 2 . . . 3 . . . 4. The answer to 2 + 2 is 4.

In other words, if you had a learning disability in mathematics, you would have to process a great deal more than would the "normal" person. You would have to translate the question, then figure out what the words meant, and then go through each step of the problem to solve it.

This takes time and energy. Furthermore, the more processing that you have to do, the more likely that you will make an error somewhere along the way.

Please understand that it isn't as if dyscalculics can't learn math or will never know what 2 + 2 is. They can and they will. It is just that they have greater difficulty thinking mathematically than do their peers.

But it isn't just math that gives them problems. Anything that requires logical thinking might be an issue. As you soon will soon see, dyscalculia can affect many aspects of your life.

CHARACTERISTICS OF INDIVIDUALS WITH DISABILITIES IN MATHEMATICS

As I have mentioned many times, individuals with learning disabilities are a diverse group. Even within specific types of learning disabilities, such as dycalculia, people may have different skills and attributes. So, describing people with learning disabilities in mathematics within a few paragraphs is challenging at best. Still, here are a few characteristics that many dyscalculics possess.

Processing, Retrieval, and Retention of Math Facts

I already talked about this briefly, but it merits repeating. Normal people are able to process questions and recall math facts so fast that they barely have to think about them. As I discuss at the beginning of the chapter, if I asked you what 2 + 2 was, you would say "4" without much thought. People with learning disabilities in mathematics don't have this quick, automatic recall. They have to process the question before attempting to come up with an answer. Moreover, they are likely to struggle when attempting to perform mathematical calculations for problems that they haven't ever encountered.

Think about what this means for a moment. A student without a learning disability is presented a problem. That student is able to quickly decipher what the equation is saying (whether it requires adding, subtracting, multiplying, etc.), pull up from memory the prerequisite knowledge, and then solve the problem.

The student is asked, "What is 2 + 2?" and in a blink of an eye, he replies "4."

The student with a learning disability, however, has to remember what a 2 is, what *plus* means, and whether the resulting answer should be bigger or smaller than the numbers that were given. Moreover, as I am about to address, the dyscalculic is likely to commit computational errors to boot! Can you see how such a student would become frustrated?

Computational Problems

One of the most noticeable characteristics of dyscalculics is that they frequently make simple computational errors. For instance, they might forget to carry remainders. Consequently, they might come up with answers like 12 + 19 = 21. Or they might confuse signs and add when they are supposed to multiply or divide when they are supposed to subtract. Or they might reverse numbers so that they answer 7 − 5 as if it were 5 − 7.

Teachers might see these errors as being merely careless mistakes or an indication that a student isn't trying or paying attention. But this usually isn't the case. Even when students with dyscalculia are motivated and trying to learn, they have a difficult time retaining the rules that govern mathematics. For example, they might habitually get the order of operations confused and solve problems from left to right. So, they might look at the problem

$$5 + 3(4 + 0)/2$$

and say that the answer is 16.

In case you have forgotten, there is something called *order of operations*, which requires that you to do certain tasks before you do others. Using this example, first you have to calculate what is in the parentheses (4 + 0). Then you have to divide what is in the parentheses by 2, which is 2. Then you multiply 2 by 3, which is 6. Finally you add the remainder (5 + 6). So, the answer is 11. But I am sure that you knew that! Students with dyscalculia might also get signs confused. For example, they might think that < means *greater than* and > means *less than*. And so forth.

Logic Problems

Computational errors and delayed processing aren't the only obstacles that people with dyscalculia experience. They also may not understand the logic behind mathematical problems. I have a story that wonderfully illustrates this point.

I had a friend who once maxed out all of her credit cards. She must have had five or six of them, each with thousands of dollars of debt. She said that she stopped using the cards and was trying to pay them off as best as she could, but she didn't make much money and couldn't afford to pay more than a little bit each month.

One day, she showed me her bill and said that the amount that she owed didn't go down as much as she had been paying each month. She would pay $20, and the total amount owed went down only $15 dollars or some such amount. She was upset and kept calling the credit card companies to get the situation corrected but to little avail.

"You are being charged interest," I explained, "which is being added to your monthly balance."

Confused, my friend looked at me and said, "But I am not using the card."

"That doesn't matter," I continued. "Every month, you are being charged interest on what you owe."

"But that is just it," she said on the verge of tears. "I owed $2,954 last month. I paid $20, and I should only owe $2,934. But this month's bill says I owe $3,261. I owe more. That can't be right!" I again explained that she was being charged interest on what she owed and that interest was more than the $20 that she was paying each month.

"At this rate," I told her, "you will never pay off the credit cards. You have to set aside more money per month if you want to reduce the debt."

Well, to make a long story short, she just couldn't wrap her mind around this concept of interest and of debts increasing at a higher rate that what she was trying to pay off. I tried using examples, such as bailing out a sinking boat with a thimble. Unless one bailed more water than what was coming into the boat, the boat would eventually sink. She didn't get it.

I tried diagramming her situation. I drew projections of how much she owed now and how much she would owe in the future. She didn't get it.

I even got out the money from *Monopoly* and started showing her how interest worked. This helped but only with a great effort on her part. I remember that she got a headache and wanted to stop talking about it.

If you are interested, my friend's car was repossessed. Her creditors took her to court and had her wages garnished. She declared bankruptcy when she was 24. Again, the point here is that mathematics matters!

Let me give you some other, less dire examples of poor logic. A student is asked the following: "Suppose that you had $10 in a piggy bank and every month you added $5 to it. How much money would you have after a year and a half had past?"

A child without a learning disability could at least guess that the correct answer is a number larger than 10. After all, you are adding to the piggy bank, not taking money away, so the answer can't be smaller than $10.

A child with a learning disability in math, however, will often not understand this logic. They don't think in terms of how the problem and the answer make sense. They just see numbers and signs and then try to solve the problem as if it were a bunch of random numbers with no meaning. So, when dyscalculics come up with an answer that doesn't fit the inherent nature of the problem (e.g., a number smaller than $10 when one is adding to $10), they may not see that it is wrong.

Spatial Reasoning

It takes a certain kind of person to really enjoy math. My father was that kind of person. He liked riddles and math problems and was able to solve things in his head. One of his abilities that truly amazed me was that he could look at a room full of furniture and boxes and know exactly how it had to go into a moving truck so that it would all fit. He didn't have to play around with the boxes or measure or even sketch out how they should go. He could just lean back, scan the room, and imagine the exact way that they needed to go.

People with dyscalculia have great difficulty doing this or anything that requires spatial reasoning. For example, look at the problem in Figure 7.1. It requires you to mentally manipulate the images in your head. A person with dyscalculia would find this challenging.

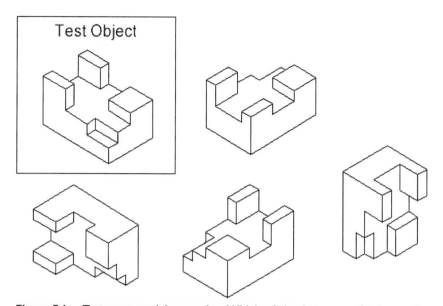

Figure 7.1. Test your spatial reasoning: Which of the four examples is *not* the same as the test object? *Source: Spatial Intelligence* (n.d.)

Shifting Mental Gears

If I were to have you write a poem and then suddenly take a math quiz, you could probably do fine on both activities. In other words, you are probably able to shift gears so that you can think of something involving language and creativity, such as writing poetry, and then do something rational and systematic, such as math.

People with dyscalculia have great problems making this shift. Thinking logically and doing math doesn't come easy to them, but shifting between expressive language and mathematical reasoning can be even harder. Let me show you how this works.

If I were to give you a mathematical formula (6/2) you could probably come up with a story that illustrates it. For example, you could say, "My friend and I had six pieces of candy, and we wanted to split them so that we each had the same amount."

In this scenario, you were able to take a mathematical problem and explain it using an example. In essence, you were able to be logical and creative at the same time. Such a task would be arduous for dyscalculics.

They would likely have problems coming up with a story that correctly illustrates the given formula.

Word Problems

Just as how people with dyscalculia struggle with explaining mathematical equations, they also have difficulty converting language into math. For example, imagine that you had the following word problem:

> You are on a blue train with 237 other people that his heading north from City A at a rate of 73 miles per hour. A red train with 429 people is heading south from City B at the rate of 64 miles per hour. How many total people are there on the two trains assuming that City A and City B are 213 miles apart?

Now, even if you hate math, I bet that you can solve this problem. You are able to examine what the question is asking (how many total people are there), locate the relevant data (429 people on the red train, plus yourself and 237 people on the blue train), and then arrive at the correct answer (667).

Because dyscalculics have trouble translating equations to language and vice versa, they may not know what the problem is asking. Furthermore, they many get distracted by all of the extraneous details (e.g., color and speed of the trains) and not know what data to focus on or even whether the problem requires addition, subtraction, multiplication, or division.

But it isn't just formal word problems that are tough for those with dyscalculia. Dyscalculics might not be able to solve everyday activities that require math or abstract reasoning. For instance, if they are at a party with 11 other people and everyone wants 3 pieces of pizza and a large pizza comes with 12 pieces, the person with dyscalculia will probably not know how many pizzas need to be ordered.

WAYS TO HELP INDIVIDUALS WITH LEARNING DISABILITIES IN MATH

Ideally, you now have a better idea about what having a learning disability in math is like. The question that you are probably asking yourself is "How do I help my child?" Here are some suggestions.

Flash Cards

There is nothing like good old-fashioned flash cards to help kids memorize their basic math facts. But you don't have to just drill and kill. You can make it fun. Make a game of it. For instance, keep track of what cards your child knows and does not know. Give points for harder cards or keep a "victory wall" where you post stickers every time your child can go through the stack without making an error.

To make flash cards beneficial, you have to use them frequently. You can't just use them until children have mastered them once. You have to keep practicing until they have committed them to memory to such a degree that they can say the correct answers without thinking. Again, the goal is to build that automated response to basic math facts. What is 2 + 2? It's 4!

Computer-Based Instruction

Speaking of making learning fun, there are tons of educational computer games out there. For example, my nephew plays a game called *Math Blaster*. I can't recall the exact plot, but basically, the player pretends to be a hero who has to fly a spaceship around the galaxy saving planets by solving math problems. I have to admit: I enjoy playing it, too.

The best feature of the game is that it keeps track of the player's highest level of achievement. So every time my nephew plays, the math questions get progressively harder and harder. Every round that he completes is like a new grade level of mathematics.

But these types of programs aren't just for little kids, nor do they focus on only rudimentary addition and subtraction. I actually bought a program for myself. You see, I was going to enter a doctoral program in economics. But I am not strong in statistics and calculus, so I bought a program that helped me review.

What was nice about my computer program was that it "talked" and gave examples. When I reviewed algebra, the program gave a 5-minute presentation on the basics, and then it gave me sample problems to work on. When I got a problem wrong, it gave me immediate feedback and explained what the correct answer was, as well as why mine was incorrect.

Manipulatives

Some people need to see and feel things to understand them. They can't just read a book or hear someone describe how to do something. They need to use hands-on activities. For such students, manipulatives are wonderful.

Manipulatives are objects that can be used to teach certain concepts. For example, when I was learning about atoms and molecules in junior high, my teacher had these blocks of wood with holes, as well as sticks that went into the holes. They were like Tinker Toys.

Anyway, my science teacher put these toys in front of us and said, "Make a water molecule." And we did. Do you know that, to this very day, I can still picture what a water molecule looks like. Well, that is, I know what it would look like if it were made out of painted Tinker Toys!

But you get my drift. Some kids need to learn math the same way. For instance, get a piece of paper and cut it into thirds or quarters or whatever you are trying to teach. Or have your child count beans, pennies, or raisins. Or have her cut up piles of Play-Doh. Rather than just have him count out loud or on his fingers, give him something that he can touch and move around. This is an excellent way to teach fractions. Students can actually see that four-fifths is bigger than three-fourths. And so on.

Real-Life, Applied Learning

Now let's put "having fun" and "manipulatives" together. Can you think of any way to teach mathematics with manipulatives that would be fun? Try thinking of activities that are applicable to real life; that way, your child will be more motivated to learn.

One strategy that comes immediately to my mind is to teach your child how to cook. Cooking takes all kinds of math skills. For example, you have to measure ingredients. You have to multiply (if you want to double your recipe) or divide (if you want to make a fraction of what the recipe calls for). You can even have your child figure out how many cookies each of his classmates would get or how many pies would have to be made for each classmate to get three slices.

Another real-life activity that uses math involves handling money. For example, one of the best assignments that I ever had when I was in school involved creating a budget. Our teacher gave us a fictitious annual salary. We then had to look in the newspaper for a place to live, and budget for rent, food, clothing, taxes, insurance, and so forth. We even invested the money that we had left into the stock market.

It was truly an incredibly educational assignment. Not only did it show us how quickly money disappears when you are an adult, but it also taught us how to balance checkbooks, estimate taxes, and how a little interest compounded regularly can grow into a big sum.

You can do something similar with your child at home. For example, you can give your daughter a weekly salary if she performs certain chores. Make sure to take out taxes. Maybe make her save a certain percentage for a long-term goal, such as college. Maybe make her save for a short-term goal, such as concert tickets. With what she has left, she can buy clothes or go to the movies or anything that she likes.

These kinds of activities teach the importance of choices and delayed gratification. After all, if the child wants something, she is going to have to work hard and save up for it. Furthermore, she has a limited income, so she has to decide what she wants most (e.g., a new car in 4 years or a new outfit now).

These activities are excellent at teaching many complex math skills in a hands-on, applied manner. Children have to perform various mathematical calculations, such as adding, subtracting, multiplying, and dividing. But they also have to understand estimations and projections (e.g., "If I save $5 per week, every week for 8 months, would I have enough to buy what I want?").

Cognitive Modeling

Cognitive modeling is a way that you can teach your child not only how to do math problems but also how not to do them. Let me explain.

When I was a kid, my father tried to help me with my math homework each night, but he wasn't a very good teacher. He certainly knew math; however, he didn't know how to convey how he was getting the answer. He would just point to a problem, $(x + 3)/2 = 8$, and say, "x equals 13." When I asked him how he got that, he would say something like "because 13 plus 3 is 16, divided by 2 is 8." This made sense. I could follow his logic, but I couldn't understand how he figured out that x equals 13.

Cognitive modeling is a way for you to verbally explain each step that you are doing to solve a problem. Using this strategy, my father should have said,

> Well, first I need to get x by itself on the lefthand side of the equal sign. I do this by doing the opposite of what each part of the problem is asking. For example, to get rid of the "divided by 2," I can multiply each side of the equation by 2. Multiplying is the opposite of dividing. So now I have x plus 3 equals 16. You see, what I did?
>
> Now I want to get rid of the "plus 3." What is the opposite of adding? Subtracting. So I want to subtract 3 from both sides. That leaves me with x equals 13.
>
> To check to see if I am right, I am going to plug 13 into the equation to see if $13 + 3$ equals 16, which it does.

In other words, cognitive modeling is kind of like thinking out loud. You explain what you are doing and why.

It is also helpful if you explain why you don't do certain things. For instance, in the aforementioned example, my father could have said, "I could have started by subtracting 3 from both sides first, but that would have been wrong because we have to go in the right order. We always start with multiplication and division problems first, and then we move to addition and subtraction." Again, the idea here is to talk through the problem and show what needs to be done and why. Don't make assumptions that your child understands why you are doing something. You have to be explicit.

After you have demonstrated a problem in this manner, have your child to do the same thing. Have him complete a math problem as he explains the process out loud. This will help you determine what mistakes he is making and why.

Schoolhouse Rock and Other Memory Aids

If you are my age, you probably remember watching *Schoolhouse Rock* every Saturday morning. If you are too young or don't recall it, *Schoolhouse Rock* was a cartoon that taught students everything from how a bill becomes a law to what conjunctions are. It did so by coming up with snappy little jingles, which have stuck in my head 20 years later—for example,

I'm just a bill,
Yes I'm only a bill,
And I got as far as Capitol Hill.
Well now I'm stuck in committee
And I sit here and wait
While a few key congressmen
Discuss and debate
Whether they should
Let me be a law . . .
Oh how I hope and pray that they will,
But today I am still just a bill. (*Schoolhouse Rock*, n.d.)

They really were terrific ways of teaching things in a fun and memorable way. If you are interested, the old *Schoolhouse Rock* songs are available on CD and DVD at any of the major commercial online outlets. There is also a *Schoolhouse Rock* website (www.schoolhouserock .tv).

The point of this section is that you can create similar jingles to help your child remember things. After all, remembering math facts is one of the difficulties that students with learning disabilities have. You don't have to create a full 3-minute song or anything like that. Just make up something that helps your child remember what she needs to remember. Let me give you a rather embarrassing example.

When I was in college, I met this woman at a party. We hit it off and wanted to get together sometime. But we didn't have pen or paper; consequently, we couldn't exchange phone numbers. So I developed this little jingle for her to remember (and, yes, I know that this is incredibly hokie):

If you need a shoulder to cry on,
Just call on me.
969-6053.

Gag! Isn't that just too stupid? At any rate, it worked. She remembered the number and called me the next day. By the way, that isn't my real number anymore, so don't bother calling it!

There are other ways to help your child to remember things. For instance, to remember the order of operations, my teachers taught me about "please excuse my dear aunt sally," which is a mnemonic devise that stands for "parentheses, exponents, multiplication, division, addition, and subtraction"—the order in which you are supposed to solve math formulae.

By going on the Internet, you should be able to find many other types of memory aids. You might also want to ask your local math teachers. They probably have books full of such strategies.

SUMMARY

In this chapter, I talk about learning disabilities in mathematics, which are sometimes referred to as *dyscalculia*. People with dyscalculia have difficulty not only in remembering how to solve math problems but also in performing spatial reasoning and verbally explaining mathematical concepts.

Moreover, people with such learning problems don't just suffer in math class. Their learning disability affects many aspects of their lives, including how to budget money, cook, and pack for a move.

8

DYSNOMIA: LEARNING DISABILITIES OF EXPRESSIVE LANGUAGE

Thus far, we have explored learning disabilities that affect reading, writing, and math. Now we will begin to investigate some areas that are often overlooked, especially by teachers.

When a student has difficulty reading, it is pretty obvious. A teacher writes something on the board and says, "What does this say?" If the student can't read it or reads it incorrectly, the teacher notices.

The same is true for writing and math. If a student has problems with adding, subtracting, or multiplying double-digit numbers or writing his name, the limitation is easy to see. Furthermore, such a student probably does poorly in English and math class.

But there are two remaining disabilities that aren't as apparent, even though they are just as common as dyslexia, dysgraphia, and dyscalculia. What are they? Well, let's go back to what the federal legislation classifies as a learning disability.

If you recall from the first pages of this book, IDEA defines *specific learning disabilities* as such:

> a disorder in one or more of the basic psychological processes involved in understanding or in using language, spoken or written, which manifest itself in imperfect ability to listen, think, speak, read, write, spell, or do mathematical calculations.

What I want to do now is talk about the "imperfect ability to . . . speak" section of this definition.

But before you begin to think about people who are mute or have paralysis in their faces and as a result have difficulty speaking, that isn't what we are going to discuss. What we are going to discuss is a condition called *dysnomia*. What is dysnomia? Ah! Excellent question!

WHAT IS DYSNOMIA?

Basically, dysnomia is a term that is often used to describe learning disabilities that affect expressive language. Let me give you an example. Suppose that you want to invite a friend to lunch at a new restaurant. So you say, "Hey, let's go out to eat at that new place."

"What place?" your friend replies.

You know the name of the restaurant. In fact, if you close your eyes, you can picture the front of the building where a large neon light is practically screaming it at you. Yet, you can't seem to get the name out of your mouth. You might say that it is on the tip of your tongue. You keep throwing out words that kind of describe the restaurant.

"You know!" you say emphatically. "That new place. It is on that street, right by that other street. It is in a building made of bricks and glass. You know, there is a light in the window. It flashes." And so it goes.

Have you ever had moments like this? You know what you want to say, but for whatever reason, you have a mental block that simply prevents you from saying it.

Let me give you another example. Remember the difference between cognitive and associative thinking, from chaper 2? Let me remind you, just in case you forgot. Cognitive thinking is when you have to actively process what you are doing. You have to concentrate to perform the activity. I used the example of learning how to drive. If you are new driver, you have to consciously think about how hard to press down on the accelerator, which direction to flip the turn signal, and so forth. However, as you become more experienced and comfortable with driving, you are able to drive without actively thinking about everything that you are doing. You drive as if you are on automatic pilot. This is called associative thinking. You do things as if they are an ingrained habit.

For most people, talking is an associative process. You know what you want to say, and you say it without much effort or concentration. In fact, you can talk and do other things at the same time, such as look around and drive your car.

However, for people with learning disabilities in expressive language (dysnomia), speaking is a cognitive process. That is, they have to focus on what they are doing in order to do it. Let me show you how this works. Next time someone comes into the room, talk with that person. Talk about anything that you like, but don't use any words that have an *h* in them. Seriously. Give it a try. It's hard, but you can do it—if you concentrate, that is. In other words, you end up speaking using a cognitive process.

Learning a foreign language is another example of using a cognitive process to speak. If you are unfamiliar with a foreign language, you have to actively focus your attention on what you want to say and how to say it. It isn't that you have a stuttering or speech problem. It is just that you have to think about what you are saying far more than a native speaker of that language does, that is, someone who speaks using an associative process.

Now, I am not saying that you have dysnomia because you occasionally have problems remembering what you want to say. That is not what I am saying at all. We all have days when our brains and mouths don't appear connected.

The difference between "normal" people and people with dysnomia is that dysnomics have to struggle far more frequently than does everyone else. Remember, according to IDEA, to have a learning disability, you have to have an impairment that is so severe that it adversely affects your ability to obtain an appropriate education. In other words, to have dysnomia, you have to have these mental blocks so habitually that you have difficulty communicating and learning.

Let's stop for a moment and think about how this would affect someone's life. After all, without that understanding, it is going to be impossible for you to truly appreciate what your child or student is going through.

Imagine that you are a kid again. However, this time around, you have dysnomia. Whenever you try to explain things to people, you frequently have great difficulty saying what you want to say. It isn't that you stutter or anything like that. Instead, you dance around the topic. How do you think your friends, teachers, and family would view you?

Many kids with dysnomia are seen as being "airheads" or "stupid." To other people, dysnomics appear to have limited vocabularies or poor attention spans. They are often misdiagnosed with the inattentive form of ADHD or even mild mental retardation.

How would this change how you grew up? Would you have more confidence in yourself? Less? Would you be more vocal? More outgoing?

Chances are that you would turn into a shy and withdrawn person. You would probably select a vocation that didn't require much interaction with other people. You are also likely to experience problems with social relationships and depression.

So although dysnomia doesn't sound as if it is that big of a deal, it can be. Again, think of all the aspects of your life that it would affect. A teacher calls on you in class to give an answer, and instead of saying "President Kennedy," you start describing what he looks like or that he was "friends" with Marilyn Monroe.

Think about trying to ask someone out for a date. You are probably nervous to begin with. Now add the fact that you have difficulty forming coherent sentences.

Think about going on job interviews. Do you think that you would do well explaining what a great employee you would be?

But there is more to dysnomia than just having difficulty spitting out what you want to say. As you will see, there are a few other critical characteristics to consider.

CHARACTERISTICS OF LEARNING DISABILITIES IN EXPRESSIVE LANGUAGE

Dysnomics share two key characteristics: difficulty with oral and written expression. Given what we have already discussed, you could have probably guessed what they were. However, for the sake of continuity, let's talk about them briefly. Then we can move on to ways that you can help individuals who have dysnomia.

Oral Expression

One of the key characteristics of dysnomics is that they have problems finding the words that they want to say. Instead of saying precisely what they want, they use vague descriptions. Moreover, they are likely to talk in a halting, disjointed manner—not stuttering, mind you, but in a manner that suggests that they are frustrated or distracted.

Another way to describe the phenomenon is to imagine someone learning a foreign language. She might know the word that she wants to say, but she has difficulty recalling how to pronounce it correctly.

Written Expression

In addition to having a tough time expressing themselves verbally, people with dysnomia may also have trouble writing what they want to say. Now this is quite different from a person who has dyslexia or dysgraphia.

Dyslexics, if you remember, have problems writing when they are copying things. They see letters that are reversed, flipped upside down, or moving. In other words, they write what they see. Dysgraphics see things fine. They have problems writing because of their hand–eye coordination. They might try to make a *d* and end up going the wrong way with the loop and instead make a *b*. Both dyslexics and dysgraphics have sloppy handwriting.

Dysnomics, however, may have a completely different issue. Their handwriting might be exquisite, and their letters might be perfect. But they may have trouble thinking of the words that they want to write. It isn't that they lack the vocabulary or don't know how to spell the words. They simply can't pull the words from their heads and then write them on the paper in front of them.

STRATEGIES TO HELP INDIVIDUALS WITH LEARNING DISABILITIES IN EXPRESSIVE LANGUAGE

So, how do you help people who have learning disabilities in expressive language? Here are a few suggestions.

Don't Interrupt

Imagine that you are speaking to someone who has a learning disability in expressive language. He is trying to tell you something but is struggling to find the correct words. What do you do?

If you are like most people, you try to "help" the person by guessing what he is trying to say. In essence, your conversation turns into a game of charades. Don't do this!

When you interrupt someone with an expressive language disability, you only make matters worse. Think about it this way. He has something in mind that he wants to say and is trying to spit it out. To "help," you start saying things and asking questions: "Do you want to go to the movies? Which movie? The one with Bruce Willis? The one with Tom Cruise?"

Now, in addition to having what he originally wanted to say in mind, he also has to try to formulate the answers to your new questions. In other words, you are adding to how much he has to process. Furthermore, you are increasing the likelihood that he is going to flounder even more.

So, when people with expressive language deficits are talking to you, don't interrupt. Don't try to finish their sentences. Don't try to guess at what they are saying. You end up just making things worse.

Give Time to Process

Instead of interrupting, give the speaker plenty of time to process what she is trying to say. This may mean that you have to wait 4 or 5 seconds longer than what you would during normal conversations.

Focus on One Topic at a Time

In addition to not interrupting and giving more time to process, try to focus on one topic at a time. For instance, my wife and I will be talking about what happened at work, and then all of a sudden, she will begin talking about what we are going to have for dinner. She often won't even indicate that she is changing topics. One moment, she will be saying,

" . . . and so Randy got in trouble for killing someone . . . ," and then the next moment she says, " . . . I think something with broccoli. What do you think?" Fortunately, I know her well enough to follow her train of thought, but she would drive someone with an expressive language disorder crazy!

Clues

If your children have expressive language difficulties, encourage them to search their memories to find clues regarding what they want to say. For example, suppose that your daughter wants to go to the movies but can't quite indicate what the name of the movie is or what time it is starting. Rather than continue to describe the movie, have your child close her eyes and see if she can picture the movie's ad that she just looked at or the marquee outside of the movie theater. Have her read or spell what she sees in her mind.

Preplanned Conversations

This is going to sound cliché; however, it is helpful to have your child think about what he wants to say before he says it. Encourage him to have all of the words sounded out in his head before he begins speaking out loud. Also encourage him to be concise and to the point.

Relaxation

Finally, much like stutters, people with learning disabilities in expressive language tend to get stressed out when they are struggling to speak. Moreover, the higher the stress level, the more problems they have speaking.

So encourage your child to practice relaxation techniques when she starts to get anxious. For example, I teach my students to use deep, cleansing breaths. Other teachers in my school use "creative visualizations," where they encourage their stressed-out students to picture themselves in a relaxing place. Again, the idea is to reduce the anxiety that may be causing a child to have difficulty communicating.

SUMMARY

In this chapter, I talk about a specific learning disability called *dysnomia*. Dysnomia adversely affects a person's expressive language abilities. People with this condition are likely to stammer over their words and have trouble saying what they want to say. It isn't that they can't pronounce the words or that there is something wrong with their mouths. It is just that they have difficulty processing what they want to say. It is much like the "tip of the tongue" phenomenon that we all experience from time to time but, for dysnomics, it is much more frequent.

9

DYSPHASIA: LEARNING DISABILITIES IN RECEPTIVE LANGUAGE

Well, here we are—talking about the last of the primary specific learning disabilities. Thus far, we have covered problems with reading, writing, math, and expressive language. What else is there?

The last condition that we are going to discuss is what I have. In case you have forgotten, not only do I have a doctorate in special education, but I also have a learning disability. What kind? I have a learning disability in receptive language.

Years back, receptive language learning disabilities were sometimes referred to as *dysphasia*, with *dys*- meaning "poor" and *-phasia* referring to "understanding speech." However, nowadays this term is mainly reserved for impairments to receptive and expressive language caused by trauma to the brain, such as that resulting from a head injury or stroke. Still, I use *dysphasia* here to be consistent with the Greek terms that I use in previous chapters (e.g., *dyslexia, dysgraphia, dysnomia*).

As you might guess, people with this kind of learning disability have problems processing what they are told. It isn't that they have hearing impairments. (Actually, I have better-than-average hearing.) And it isn't that they aren't paying attention. They simply have difficulty processing auditory information.

Imagine having this problem. Think about how it would affect you and your life. People would probably think that you were spacey, inattentive, or unmotivated to remember things. As with other learning disabilities, you might be misdiagnosed with other conditions, such as ADHD.

But what exactly is dysphasia, or receptive language learning disabilities? If it isn't caused by a hearing loss, what is going on?

WHAT IS DYSPHASIA?

When I talk about learning disabilities in reading (in chapter 5), I discuss how dyslexics have a tough time processing what they see. It isn't that they have a vision impairment. Their visual acuity might actually be better than 20/20. However, they have abnormalities in their brains that makes processing written words challenging. Consequently, they might see letters inverted or moving.

When I talk about learning disabilities in written language, I discussed how dysgraphics struggle with hand–eye coordination. They might want to draw a *W*, but their hands end up creating an *M*. Again, there is nothing wrong with their eyes or their hands. Their brains simply work a bit differently from what is considered normal.

The same is true for people like myself who have learning disabilities in receptive language. We might hear perfectly fine, but we don't process auditory stimuli very efficiently.

The best way that I can illustrate this is to have you imagine that you are listening to someone who is speaking a foreign language. Assume that you know the foreign language but only at a cursory level. You have the basic vocabulary down, but you have to really concentrate to understand what that person is saying. Moreover, when someone says something, you have to translate it back into your native language. To me, this is how the world is.

I speak English fluently. It is my native language. However, when people talk to me, I frequently have to really focus on what they are saying. I have to translate what they are telling me so that I can understand it.

Names and numbers are particularly problematic. If you tell me your name, it stays in my working memory for only a few second before it disappears. It is like smoke in the wind. It is there one moment and gone the next.

When people leave their phone numbers on my answering machine, I have to play their messages over and over again before I can write down their complete numbers. For example, someone might leave a message saying, "Hi, Rob. This is your agent. Give me a call at 9-8-7-9-9-9-3-2-1-0." When I hear the numbers, I have to translate what they are. So when my agent says the word *nine*, I have to stop and think, "Oh, that is a '9'—got it." But by the time I can visually picture what a the number 9 is, he has already finished his message.

This happens frequently but not with everything that I hear. When my agent leaves such a message, I don't have to translate the "Hi, Rob" part. I have heard that so often that it is easy for me to process. But anything unfamiliar, such as new vocabulary, names, or numbers, requires considerable concentration for me to understand.

Let me state this another way. For "normal" people, listening is an associative process. You are probably able to read this book, listen to your kids scream a question from across the house, and scream an answer back, all at the same time. For me, listening is a cognitive process. I have to think about what is being said. I have to consciously process the words to make sense of them, especially if the topic of the conversation is new or unfamiliar or if it deals with a lot of numbers.

CHARACTERISTICS OF INDIVIDUALS WITH LEARNING DISABILITIES IN RECEPTIVE LANGUAGE

I hope that you have a general feel for what it is like to have a learning disability in receptive language. Let's talk a little bit about some of the key characteristics that are common with this condition.

Poor Auditory Memory

As I have described, people with learning disabilities in receptive language have poor auditory memories. They simply don't retain what they hear. Again, this is caused by an abnormality with the parts of the brain that process auditory information. In other words, people like me don't have hearing impairments.

Distinguishing Sounds

People with learning disabilities in receptive language also have problems distinguishing sounds. For example, when I was learning Spanish in college, I had a horrible time telling the difference between *cerveza* (beer) and *cabeza* (head). They sound exactly the same to me. Some of my students who have receptive language learning disabilities report that they can't hear the difference between such words as *pin* and *pen* or *pet* and *pat.*

Reproducing Sounds

In addition to facing difficulty in distinguishing sounds, people with learning disabilities in receptive language often find it challenging to reproduce sounds or say certain words. For example, I can't say *aluminum* or *gracious.* I don't know why. It is as if I can't hear the words correctly in my head, so I can't reproduce them.

Now, I am different from people who have dysnomia and are having problems recalling the words that they want to say. I know that I want to say *aluminum* or *gracious.* I simply can't make the sounds that compose the words.

STRATEGIES TO HELP INDIVIDUALS WITH LEARNING DISABILITIES IN RECEPTIVE LANGUAGE

So, that is what learning disabilities in receptive language are like. The question remains, how can you help your child if she or he has this condition? Here are a few strategies that might help.

Repeating

Whenever I have to remember something that I have been told, I repeat it several times. For instance, if I meet someone and I have to remember her name, I repeatedly mention it. I might say, "It is good to meet you, Suzie" and "So, Suzie, what do you do for a living?" And so forth. The more that I say "Suzie," the easier it is for me to remember it.

Of course, I also repeat information that I need to remember to myself. For example, the other day, I was walking to a meeting when someone stopped and told me that it had been moved to a different room. The person told me the new location, and I had to keep saying "210B . . . 210B . . . 210B," or else I would have forgotten.

Chunking

One of the reasons why it is so hard for people like me to remember what they are told is that they try to remember every piece of information in isolation. For example, when I have to remember the phone number (987) 654-3210, I say to myself, "Okay, 9 comes first, followed by an 8, then a 7 . . . " In other words, I am attempting to remember not only 10 numbers but also the order in which they were said. That is a lot to remember.

Instead, it is far easier to remember larger patterns of information. For instance, the sample phone number is really the numbers 9 to 0, in descending order. That's easy to recall. Let me give you another example. Try to commit the following letters to memory in their correct order:

ACA
TSI
TSO
NTH
EWI
NDO
WSI
LL

How difficult was it? If you realized that the letters spelled something (*A cat sits on a windowsill*), memorizing it was probably pretty easy. After all, you only had to remember six words. However, if you tried to remember each letter, you had 23 things to retain. Do you see the point that I am trying to make? It is much easier for you to remember pieces of information that have been grouped together than to remember each letter. This strategy is called *chunking*. Let me demonstrate it one more time.

Consider the information *1986FAQB2Z*. I just made that up. My fingers hit random keys. How would you try to remember this series of letters and numbers? I would chunk them into three groups. I would first remember *1986*, which was the year that I graduated high school; then *FAQ*, which stands for "frequently asked questions"; and then *B2Z*. So rather than recall 10 pieces of data, I have to remember only 3. Furthermore, I have assigned some meaning to the first two chunks, which will help me recall them. So, all I have to remember is the year I graduated high school (1986), "frequently asked questions" (such questions are natural to have after graduating high school), and B2Z. See how that works?

Visualizing

Another strategy that I use involves visualizing what I have been told. This helps me a great deal, especially with names. When I have to remember someone's name, say, Wayne, I mentally picture the word *Wayne* underneath an image of Wayne's face. I conjure up a portrait of the person with his name written on the frame. Once I see something, I am more likely to remember it.

Air Drawing

In addition to mentally picturing something, I also draw in the air what I am trying to remember. This might sound a bit silly, so let me explain.

If you are telling me directions to get to your house, you might say, "Go down this street and take the third left. Then go one block, take a right, and go for a mile and a half. Then take another left. My house is the third house on the right."

With all of those *right*'s and *left*'s and with *one* this and *one and a half* that and *third* whatever, I would get completely and utterly lost. I simply can't retain all of this information, let alone in the correct order. I would probably end up going down the street for a mile and a half and look for a house on my left!

So what I do is trace the route in the air. I have my finger stop-and-go three times in a straight line, then have it turn left, and so on. This not only helps me see the route but also feel it. The movement of my hand, such as its starting and stopping three times, reminds me that I have to go three blocks before turning left.

This is called *muscle memory*. It is how we are able to find our way to the bathroom in the middle of the night without turning on the light. Our bodies recall how many steps we have to take before we reach the hallway and so forth.

Write It Down

Of course, the best strategy for me is to actually write things down. Because I can't remember what I am told, I carry a little pad of paper and a short "golf" pencil in my back pocket (you know, those little pencils with no erasers that you get at the golf course or mini-putt-putt). If people want to schedule a meeting with me or something, I write it down while they are there.

My colleagues, who realize that I have a really poor auditory memory, make sure that I write things down before they leave me. Otherwise, there is a good chance that I will forget whatever it is that I was told.

Show Me

Whenever possible, I try to have people show me things rather than tell me. E-mail has been a godsend in this respect. If a student wants something from me, I ask him or her to send me an e-mail. If I read something, I tend to remember. The same is true for my remembering how to do certain things. For example, a few days ago, I asked someone how to make a spreadsheet on our new computer program. She started to explain how to do it.

"You just go up to the 'Edit' menu, click, and highlight 'Create' . . . " she began.

I knew that that wasn't going to work. There were already too many steps for me to remember. So I had my friend sit down at a computer and show me what to do. Once I saw what she did, I got it right away. I didn't need any more help.

Reproducing Similar Sounds

Whenever I can't say a word, I try to break it down into more manageable sounds. For example, *aluminum* can be reduced to *al-lou-men-um*, all of which I can say. Of course, it takes some rehearsing, so I don't say it like Frankenstein would, all slow and fragmented; but, eventually, I get the hang of it.

SUMMARY

There are many types of specific learning disabilities. The type of learning disability that your child has often dictates the help that he or she will need. For example, if your child has a learning disability in receptive language, she will undoubtedly have trouble processing information that is told to her. She may also have difficulty reproducing sounds or learning new words.

In this chapter, I talk about what it is like to have a receptive language learning disability. I stress that the underlying problem isn't a hearing loss. So, hearing aids or speaking louder isn't going to help. Instead, you might want to try some of the strategies that I outline here in order to help someone with a receptive language learning disability.

10

GENERAL ISSUES TO CONSIDER WHEN WORKING WITH CHILDREN WITH LEARNING DISABILITIES

Well, we are approaching the end of our time together. Thus far, we have talked about what learning disabilities are; how they should be diagnosed; and how to help individuals with specific conditions, such as dyslexia, dysgraphia, and dyscalculia. What I want to do now is focus on some topics that apply to all children with learning disabilities, regardless of their specific diagnoses. Much of what I am about to discuss will undoubtedly sound like common sense, but you would be surprised at how, for some people, it is not.

For instance, many of the parents with whom I have worked have not saved money for their children's college education. Evidently, they thought that their children wouldn't be able to get into college because of their learning disabilities. That is to say, the parents believed that college is too tough for those with learning disabilities and that such students wouldn't even get accepted into a college program. When these parents realized their mistake, their children were unable to go to college because of financial, not academic, reasons.

Again, it probably sounds like common sense when I say to you, "Prepare as if your child is going to go to college." But ask around. I bet most of the parents whom you know who have children with learning disabilities don't make such preparations. Parents of "normal" kids, however, start saving as soon as their children are born, if not earlier.

So, just relax, sit back, and read the next few pages with an open mind. Think about your own situation and make sure that you don't dismiss anything out of hand or because you think, "I already do that."

FIND OUT WHAT KIND OF LEARNING DISABILITY YOUR CHILD HAS

As hard as it is for me to believe, most teachers and parents have no idea what kind of learning disabilities their children have. When I ask them, they usually say something like "Oh, he just has a general learning disability" or "She has a severe learning disability." Ugh!

How can these parents and teachers expect to help their children if they don't even know what kind of learning difficulties their children have? It is like saying that a blind person has a "sensory impairment" and then teaching him as if he were deaf. It makes no sense.

As I say at the beginning of the book, you need to find out what kind of learning disability your child has. This is so incredibly important. If the person who evaluated your child doesn't know, then get a different evaluator. Get someone who actually knows something about learning disabilities.

You simply must know in what areas your child is struggling and why. For example, don't merely accept that your child has difficulty with writing. You need to know why she is struggling with writing. Is it that she has dyslexia and sees things moving around? Does she have dysgraphia and writes poorly because of poor hand–eye coordination? Does she have dysnomia and can't recall what she wants to say? You and your child's teachers cannot help your child without first understanding what the underlying problem is.

DETERMINE YOUR CHILD'S LEARNING STYLE

In addition to knowing what kind of learning disability your child has, you also need to figure out how your child learns best. That is, how does your child processes information most efficiently? Is he a visual learner, like I am? Does he remember things that he sees and reads? Or does he prefer to hear things and is thus an auditory learner? Or does he have to physically touch and manipulate objects to see how they work? And so forth.

Without knowing how your child learns best, you are really teaching with one hand tied behind your back. Not every kid is a visual learner or a haptic learner. If you don't know your child's learning style, ask the person who diagnosed her with a learning disability. Even ask your child. If she doesn't know, ask for another assessment. In the meantime, try different teaching techniques and see which works best.

FOCUS ON THE ULTIMATE GOAL

I am not about to sit here and tell you how to raise your child. I don't want to do that at all. But I do want to make you stop and think for a few minutes about your goals and what you want your child to accomplish. For example, are good grades really that important? Now before you say yes, hear me out for a second.

There is this fallacy that grades measure knowledge. They don't. Grades measure a bunch of things, including whether a student turns in homework on time, participates in class, and gets along with the teacher. There is also this belief that kids have to do well in school to do well in life. Although it is true that doing well in school doesn't hurt your future, it doesn't guarantee your success.

Take me, for example. I was a C student in high school. Actually, I frequently got D's. I even failed Spanish. But I ended up earning a doctorate by the time I was 27. I am not saying that getting a PhD is somehow the mark of success and that people who don't get such a degree are less successful than those who do. Personally, I measure success through accomplishing personal goals. For instance, I wanted to earn a doctorate, write books, and teach college, and that is what I do. Your child might want to do something completely different, such as become a veterinarian who treats sick farm animals and breeds race horses. Helping her accomplish those goals is helping her to succeed.

At any rate, my point is this: Grades don't predict success. As a matter of fact, there have even been studies indicating that one's high school grade point average isn't strongly correlated with achievement in college or even with college completion.

So take a moment and consider how you define success. In other words, what exactly do you want your child to be like when he grows up? Do you want him to be smart? rich? famous? happy? creative? honest? loyal? caring?

Now, if you said yes to everything, aren't you putting a lot of pressure on your child? I mean, who can be all of that? How well adjusted would you be if your parents expected you to be a rich and famous happy person who is really creative, honest, loyal, and caring? How would you feel if you weren't a couple of those things, such as famous? Would you feel as if you let your parents down?

Rather than expect your child to be everything that is good in the world, maybe you should focus on one or two characteristics that you believe are critical. For instance, maybe your main desire is to have your child make a positive difference in the world. Or maybe you just want your child to be happy, adhere to a certain religion, or be active in the community. Again, it is up for you to decide how to measure success.

However, I am not saying that you should let your child skip school and fail out of third grade because you want him to be happy. I am not saying that at all. I am just saying that a lot of parents put a tremendous amount of stress on their children about grades, athletic ability, popularity, and so forth, when other things are probably more important. Remember, kids with learning disabilities tend to have other issues, such as depression and anxiety. Maybe these are more important than academics or appearance.

Perhaps, I am beating a dead rhinoceros or something, but as someone with a learning disability, I really wish that my parents and teachers would have focused on how hard I tried rather than on what grades I brought home. I never was a very good student. It took a lot of effort for me to learn. If they would have reinforced my effort rather than punish me for my poor grades, I think that I would have done better and been happier.

Enough said.

DON'T LET LEARNING DISABILITIES BECOME AN EXCUSE

Another important suggestion that I have is to not let your child use his or her learning disability as an excuse for not trying. I think that this is incredibly crucial. I can't stress it enough.

Far too often, I see students, especially high school and college students, who use their disabilities as a means to get out of doing work or to lower their teachers' expectations. For example, a while back, I had a student come up to me and say that she was going to need more time to do an assignment. When I asked why, she said that she had a learning disability. What really bothered me about this was that it was only the second or third week of the class and the project wasn't due until the end of the semester. She had 11 or 12 weeks to do a project that could have been completed in a couple of days. She didn't even try to complete the project on time. She didn't even start. And she was already claiming that she couldn't get it done.

Furthermore, many of my college students who have learning disabilities try to get around various rules and regulations by using their learning disabilities coupled with threats of lawsuits. For instance, to stay in our program, students must maintain a certain grade point average. I think that it is a 2.75 out of a 4.00 scale. Basically, students must get at least C-pluses in their classes.

We have one student who has a cumulative grade point average well below the cutoff. I think her GPA is 1.80 or something like that. So, she was sent a letter saying that if she didn't get her average up, she wouldn't be allowed to complete her degree. The student raised all kinds of hell. She said that she had a learning disability and that it was harder for her to learn and that the grade requirements should not apply to her. She even threatened to sue the university.

I know this student. She has been in four of my classes, in which she earned two C's, a D, and an F. But these grades have nothing to do with her learning disability. They have everything to do with her motivation. You see, she showed up only 4 out of 16 times. This includes the final exam! Moreover, she never turned in a homework assignment on time. Frankly, she gets low grades because she doesn't care.

Somewhere along the line, this student and many others like her decide that they don't have to try to learn and that if anybody calls them on their lack of motivation, they are going to play the "disability card." This is a shame. Not only does it limit their potential, but it also creates a negative opinion of people with learning disabilities in general.

I am not saying that students with learning disabilities shouldn't get accommodations. They should, if they need them. However, students shouldn't use their learning disabilities as a way of getting out of doing work or lowering the quality of the work that they are expected to do.

So, what can you do to help address this issue? First of all, I strongly encourage you to instill accountability into your child. Remember, people with learning disabilities are people who happen to learn differently from the norm. But they are still people and, as such, should adhere to all of the rules and expectations that everyone else does.

Second, encourage your child to attempt activities and schoolwork without any accommodations. Then, if your child needs modifications or extra help, have him ask his teacher. But he should at least try to do the work just as any other student would.

Finally, stress to your child that she is expected to do something with her life and that people with learning disabilities can succeed. We've talked about this before, but it is certainly important enough to warrant repeating. Have your child read biographies of famous people who have learning disabilities. Have her join support groups or professional organizations where she can meet people just like her who are successful. Do whatever you can to get your child to understand that learning disabilities don't mean "stupid."

PLAN FOR THE FUTURE, BUT BE FLEXIBLE

As I mention at the beginning of this chapter, many parents of children with learning disabilities don't plan for their children's future—at least not in the same way that parents of "normal" children plan. Earlier, I use the example of saving money for college. Many of my students' parents didn't think that their kids could go to college because of their learning disabilities, so they stopped saving. Furthermore, they stopped reinforcing the idea that going to college was an expectation.

I think that part of this lack of planning is the fault of teachers, myself included. We spend so much of our time focusing on the here and now and not enough time looking at long-term issues. After all, as I talk about in the next chapter, teachers don't begin to really start talking about life after school until the child is around 14 years old. We need to begin doing so before this age.

Help your child plan for her future, but be flexible. By this, I mean, realize that goals change over time. When your child is in middle school, she may not want to go to college. Still, you should start preparing just in case she changes her mind. Start saving money. Have her take the classes that she will need to get into college.

CHALLENGE YOUR CHILD

Whatever you do, please challenge your child. This ties into what we talked about earlier regarding how learning disabilities shouldn't be an excuse for not trying. Let me tell you a quick story.

A friend of mine has a stepdaughter, Ada, who was really worried about taking Spanish in high school. Ada has a learning disability and poor self-esteem. She rarely takes a risk and tries something new. Consequently, she didn't want to take Spanish because she thought that she was going to fail. Sound familiar?

However, her parents wanted her to take Spanish because many colleges require at least one semester of a foreign language in high school. So, my friend said to her stepdaughter, "Look, take Spanish, do your best, and if you fail . . . I won't get angry. I promise. At least you tried."

My friend was sincere about this. She just wanted her stepdaughter to try. The final grade didn't matter.

Not only did Ada get a B-plus in Spanish, but she took two more semesters and ended up majoring in Spanish at the University of Wisconsin!

The moral, of course, is that you never know what you are capable of until you try. Sometimes, we have to push children with learning disabilities to try. After all, as I mention in the fourth chapter, they don't like taking risks. But if you focus on their efforts rather than on the final outcomes, taking risks becomes less scary and much easier for them.

SHOULD YOU TELL YOUR CHILD
ABOUT HIS OR HER CONDITION?

Whenever I present at conferences or put on workshops, people always seem to ask me this question: "Should I tell my child about his or her learning disability?" You see, many parents are worried that they are going to cause their children to have anxiety or make them feel bad by telling them the results of their nondiscriminatory evaluation. But I always say, "Yes, tell them!" This is why.

Imagine being a kid. You have been struggling in school most of your life. One day, you take a bunch of tests, but no one tells you what the results are or what they mean. They just make you periodically leave your regular education classroom to learn with the "dumb" kids down the hall. If you are like most children, you probably feel a bit confused and frustrated, maybe even angry and resentful or powerless. Don't you want to know what is going on?

If you are still unsure, consider this question: How can we help teach children to learn more effectively if we don't tell them what their problem is? I mean, think about it. Your child has a hard time reading. She has dyslexia and sees letters moving all over the place. She probably just naturally assumes that everyone else does as well. Furthermore, she probably thinks that she is too stupid to figure out what the words mean.

What I am saying is that many kids experience a great deal of relief when they learn that they have a disability. I know that I did. When I was told that I had ADHD and an auditory learning disability, I didn't get depressed and cry to the heavens, "Why me?!" I was happy. I was ecstatic, actually. For the first time in my life, I realized why I was so different. I wasn't stupid after all. I just had a learning disability. No big deal.

There is something else that you need to consider. Being diagnosed with ADHD and a learning disability made me feel part of a larger community. There were support groups, chat rooms, and other people with whom I could share my experiences and learn from. This is going to sound strange, but my having a learning disability is much like my being Norwegian. It is part of who I am. When I meet another person with ADHD or a learning disability, I feel at home and comfortable. That person gets me better than any "normal" person does.

A lot of "normal" people don't understand that. They are so anti-labeling that they don't understand how much comfort having that label gives someone like me. Let me see if I can explain this better.

Imagine going up to someone who is a minority in some way. Maybe that person is African American or Jewish or gay. Now would you ever try to convince such a person that his or her background wasn't important? Would you ever say to an African American, "You know, African Americans are basically White people with darker skin. So I am going to just forget your heritage and treat you like any of my White friends." Would you say that? No.

The fact is that I, like a lot of people, have a learning disability, and that learning disability is a large part who I am and who we are. Deny the importance or the significance of my disability, and you deny me. You minimize what I have gone through and felt my entire life.

So I say, tell your children about their learning disabilities, and encourage them to be happy with who they are. But this is just my opinion. You are welcome to your own.

The question then becomes, how should you tell children about their learning disabilities? My first suggestion is, don't make a big deal about it. You don't need to call a family meeting, look your child sadly in the face, and say, "Honey, we have something to tell you. You have a . . . LEARNING DISABILITY!!!" After all, you don't want to create a negative impression. Learning disabilities aren't bad. They aren't character flaws. They are just part of what a person is.

The following is how I explain learning disabilities to young kids; perhaps, this will help you. I talk with the children about their classmates. One on one, I say things like "I bet there is someone in your class who is really good at kickball."

This will usually agree and tell me all about the star kickballer in his or her class.

Then I say, "And I bet there is someone who is really good at spelling."

Again, the student usually agrees and tells me all about Susie or Hector or whoever is good at spelling.

"And I bet that there is someone in your class who is really funny and can tell all kinds of jokes and make everyone laugh."

This usually results in a 10-minute tangent where the student retells all of the funny things that the class clown did that week.

"You see," I explain, "everyone is good at something. Some people are good at playing kickball. Some are good at spelling. Some are good at telling jokes. But no one is good at everything.

"You are good at a great many things." And here I list the student's strengths.

"But you need help in x, y, z . . . just like the class clown probably needs help with spelling or playing kickball.

"My job is to figure out how you learn best and then to teach you and your teachers how to use those strengths to make you even better than you already are, just like how I might help other students be better in math or science or spelling or kickball."

I try not to mention the word *disability*. Instead, I talk about differences and that everyone is different in some way. I also try to talk about the student's strengths and how the student can use those strengths to excel. Again, I try to make the entire conversation honest (the student already knows that he or she has a problem) but also positive (no one is good at everything and that is okay).

SUMMARY

In previous chapters, I talk about how to help individuals with specific learning disabilities, such as dyslexia or dysnomia. In this chapter, I cover a few important concepts that relate to everyone, regardless of the type of learning disabilities that one has. For example, I strongly encourage you to challenge your child, as well as not to let him or her use the disability as an excuse not to try.

In the next chapter, I talk about special education and your rights as a parent. Once you know your rights, you can put some of the suggestions that we have discussed throughout this entire book into practice, not only at home, but at school as well.

THE RIGHTS OF PARENTS OF
CHILDREN IN SPECIAL EDUCATION

Well, our time together is almost at an end. I hope that by now you have a good understanding about what learning disabilities are, how they are diagnosed, what kinds of learning disabilities are out there, and how to address some of the problems associated with them. I suppose that we could just stop here and part company, but I think that we have a little bit more to talk about.

You see, you might know more about learning disabilities than when you first picked up this book. But you won't be able to help your child if you don't know how to utilize what you have learned. In this chapter, I want to talk briefly about what special education is and what your rights are as a parent of a child with a disability. Once you understand special education and its rules, you will be better able to work with school personnel to improve your child's future.

As with any legal issues, the topics that I am about to discuss can fill volumes of thick texts. Of course, I can't go into that kind of depth here, so I am just going to go over some of the most significant nuances that you will undoubtedly face. If you require additional information, please consult the resources in the back of this book or contact a lawyer whose specialty is disability law.

WHAT IS SPECIAL EDUCATION?

The best place to start our discussion is with the question "What is special education?" After all, although it is a common-enough term, few laypeople really understand it. In fact, if you say *special education* to the average person, what probably comes to mind are images of kids in wheelchairs who have profound mental retardation or cerebral palsy. Although kids with profound mental retardation and cerebral palsy who use wheelchairs can certainly be associated with special education, they hardly give you a good representation of what special education is.

So, what is special education? Well, simply put, it is a federally mandated entitlement program for children between the ages of 3 and 21 who have a qualifying disability that adversely affects their ability to achieve an appropriate education. There is a ton of information in that sentence, so let me break it down into manageable chunks.

Federally Mandated

All schools that receive state and federal funds have to have special education programs, and that, of course, includes all public schools. Some private schools are also required to have programs for students with disabilities, if they have federal or state grants. If your child is attending a private school and you want to know whether it accepts federal funds, just ask. It is a matter of public record, so a school representative should tell you without balking.

Entitlement Program

In addition to being federally mandated, special education is an entitlement program. That is to say, if your child qualifies for special education, she or he cannot be denied services or kicked out. So, if your school district can't afford to provide services to your child or if the one and only special education teacher quit just a couple days ago—too bad. The school still must furnish your child specialized services.

Children Between the Ages of 3 and 21

This part is probably self-explanatory. However, there are two important pieces of information here that I want to point out. First, special education services can begin when a child turns 3 years old. Therefore, your child could receive services before he or she actually enters school. In fact, there are all kinds of early prevention and intervention programs that can help young children with disabilities. Granted, most of these services are given to children with pretty severe disabilities, such as profound mental retardation and acute physical impairments, because they are diagnosed shortly after birth. Your child probably won't get these kinds of services. Still, it is important to note that special education begins at such an early age. It is also important to note that special education continues until the student is 21 years old. As soon as students turn 21, they can be "aged out" of school—that is, services end.

I know many parents who keep their children in school a little longer than usual. For instance, one family with whom I have worked has a son with a learning disability. Academically, he was far behind his peers, so they kept him in high school until he was 19. He got a year of extra education and then went to college.

Qualifying Disabilities

The next phrase that we need to look at is *qualifying disabilities*. You might be surprised to learn that not all kids with disabilities are entitled to special education. In fact, relatively few children with disabilities can actually access special education services. To be one of the elite, a student must have one of the disabilities listed in Table 11.1. The numbers listed to the right indicate the percentages of students composing special education.

As you can see, specific learning disabilities are the most common disability served via special education programs. A little more than half of all children served in special education programs have one of the learning disabilities discussed earlier. However, just because one has a listed disability doesn't guarantee that one can enroll in special education. One has to have another condition. What is that other condition? Ah! Stay tuned.

Table 11.1.   Percentages of Students in Special Education, by Disability

Specific learning disabilities	51.0%
Speech or language impairments	19.8
Mental retardation	11.2
Emotional behavioral disturbance	8.4
Other health impairments	3.5
Multiple disabilities	2.0
Hearing impairments	1.3
Orthopedic impairments	1.2
Autism	0.8
Vision impairments	0.5
Traumatic brain injury	0.2
Developmental delay	< 0.1
Deaf/blindness	< 0.1

Source: U.S. Department of Education (2006)

Adversely Affect Ability to Receive an Appropriate Education

In addition to having 1 of the 11 conditions listed in the table, your child's disability must also be so severe that her ability to receive an "appropriate" education is adversely affected. In other words, your child might have a learning disability, but because she is still able to receive an appropriate education without supports, she is not entitled to special education.

You are probably thinking, "What is an 'appropriate' education?" Well . . . that is a toughie. There is no real cut-and-dried answer. Basically, if a student can make adequate progress through the general education curriculum without support, she isn't entitled to special education.

"What is 'adequate' progress?" you might persist.

Again, there is no real concrete answer. But maybe I can give you some examples to at least give you an idea. Let's suppose that your child is super smart. I mean, she is close to the top of her class, is on the honor roll, and is taking college-level courses. You are very proud.

Let's also suppose that your child has a learning disability. Perhaps, she has dyscalculia and isn't as good in math as she should be; however, she is still getting B's in her math classes. With a little extra help, you believe that she can get straight A's.

If you were to attempt to get special education services for your daughter, you would probably be denied. Why? Because she is already making adequate progress through the general education curriculum without any help. After all, she is getting B's in her worst subject. That isn't too bad!

What if she were getting all C's? Or maybe some C's and a few D's? Would she qualify for special education then?

Well, it depends on what the M-team thinks. Recall that the M-team (the multidisciplinary team) assesses your child and then determines whether she has a disability. They also decide whether your child's disability is severe enough to prevent her from getting an appropriate education without services. I have a story that might illustrate how subjective all of this is.

Recently, I testified in a case where a child was being denied access to special education. School officials stated that the child didn't have a learning disability, because he was getting mostly A's in his classes. In essence, the school was saying, "Your child doesn't have a learning disability, because he is already getting an appropriate education." I was called in as an expert witness by the student's family.

After assessing the student, I found that his abilities were nowhere near that of his peers. He is in high school and reading at a fourth-grade level. I further found that that his schoolwork didn't warrant the A's that he was receiving. He was in an English literature class, allegedly reading books by Mark Twain. But the answers on his tests weren't even close to being correct, even though he got passing grades. In other words, his teachers were giving him A's so that it would look as if his disability didn't adversely affect his education. Therefore, he didn't officially qualify for special education.

In the end, the hearing officer sided with the family (I'll talk about what a hearing officer is later). The student is now getting special education services. Unfortunately, he is still in a school with low standards for ethical conduct.

WHAT DOES SPECIAL EDUCATION ACTUALLY DO?

So that is what special education is. Now let's talk about what it can do for your child. The philosophy behind special education is really twofold.

First, it attempts to teach children with disabilities the general education curriculum as much as possible. That means that your child is supposed to be taught the same things as his peers as much as is reasonably possible. Notice that we are talking about what is being taught, not how. Although one of the goals of special education is to teach your child everything that his nondisabled peers are learning, the method of how your child is instructed can differ dramatically from regular education to special education.

For instance, maybe your child is supposed to learn double-digit addition in his second-grade regular education class. Even though your child is in special education, he should still be taught double-digit addition. But he might be taught double-digit addition differently from how his nondisabled peers are. His peers might be shown flash cards whereas your child might utilize a multisensory approach or a computer program. The strategy that is employed depends on the learning needs of your child.

The second philosophical underpinning of special education involves where children with disabilities are taught. Specifically, IDEA mandates that special education students be taught in the least restrictive environment (LRE) as appropriate.

Notice that I wrote *as appropriate*. Many people erroneously believe that IDEA says that all children with disabilities have to be taught in the regular education classroom alongside their nondisabled peers. That simply isn't true.

Although the goal of special education is to teach children with disabilities as "normally" as possible, it doesn't mean that all children belong in the regular education classroom. In fact, there are many students who don't belong in the same school as typical students. Let me give you a few examples.

One of my colleagues had a student in her elementary school class named Tim, who had an imaginary friend named Mr. Headache. Mr. Headache used to talk to Tim and tell him to do things, such as yell and scream and bother other students. And if Tim didn't do what he was told, Mr. Headache would cause him pain.

At first, Tim's teachers thought that that he was only acting. However, when Mr. Headache started to tell Tim to kill animals, they knew that he was a sick and troubled little boy. As smart as Tim was, he didn't belong in the regular education classroom or the regular school. He was placed in a psychiatric hospital for children where he was treated for early-onset schizophrenia and was taught everything that other kids were taught.

Tim is now doing much better. Mr. Headache is controlled with medications, but Tim still has some significant issues with social skills and impulsivity. He is presently taught in a self-contained classroom in his local public school with other children diagnosed with behavior disorders.

I could give many other examples of students who shouldn't have been taught in the regular education classroom. For instance, several of my former students were sexual predators. They exposed themselves and molested other kids. I also had a student who killed his family with a hatchet. These students were taught in a lockdown residential facility.

The point is that children in special education are supposed to be treated just like children without disabilities. And most are. Most are taught alongside their nondisabled peers, but there are exceptions.

Take a look at the numbers in Table 11.2. As you can see, nearly half of all special education students are taught in the regular classroom for the majority of their day. Only about 4% are taught in completely separate schools or facilities. As for students with learning disabilities, even more of them are taught alongside their peers (see Table 11.3).

You are probably wondering, "How do I decide where my child should be taught?" After all, you are on the IEP team, and the IEP team decides where your child's LRE is. How do you decide?

There is no definite way to determine a student's LRE. At least, there is nothing written in IDEA about how such a thing is accomplished. However, there is a certain procedure that most special educators seem to follow. It goes something like this.

Table 11.2. Percentages of Special Education Students, by Time Spent in Regular Classrooms or Otherwise

In regular education more than 80% of the time	48%
In regular education between 40% and 80% of the time	28
In regular education less than 40% of the time	20
In separate schools	3
In nonacademic facilities (e.g., hospitals, detention facilities, etc.)	1

Source: U.S. Department of Education (2001)

Table 11.3.   Percentages of Students With Learning Disabilities, by Time Spent in Regular Classrooms or Otherwise

In regular education more than 80% of the time	45%
In regular education between 40% and 80% of the time	38
In regular education less than 40% of the time	15
In separate schools	1
In nonacademic facilities (e.g., hospitals, detention facilities, etc.)	1

Source: U.S. Department of Education (2001)

First, you consider placing your child in the regular education environment, with no modification, changes, or assistance. Then you ask yourself, "Can my child obtain an 'appropriate' education like this?" Chances are, you are going to say, "No." After all, if she can get an appropriate education in the regular education classroom without any help, then she wouldn't be in need of special education.

So then you ask yourself, "What does my child need to get an appropriate education and be in the regular education classroom full-time?" You might make a list. For example, she may need extra time to take tests, guided class notes provided by the teacher before lectures, and shortened assignments in math or reading or whatever subjects she is having problems with.

Now consider whether those accommodations, services, and modifications are reasonable. That is, if the teacher did everything that you asked, would the rest of the students suffer? Or is what you are asking completely impossible within the confines of a 7-hour school day? If what you are asking for is reasonable and the rest of the IEP team agrees, then you have found your child's LRE. If you believe that you have come up with a reasonable solution but the other members of the IEP team disagree, then you can take the school to what is called a *due process hearing*. We'll talk about that later.

But let's suppose that your child is really far behind in various subjects and that, for her to catch up, she is going to need a lot more direct instruction than would be possible in a regular class of 28 other children. Maybe you want her to get intensive one-on-one instruction with a reading teacher or some other specialist. Furthermore, she needs to be taught at the third-grade level rather than at the fifth. So you are worried that she will feel self-conscious if the other kids saw her doing work that is below them.

In this situation, maybe you feel that being fully included in regular education isn't appropriate. Perhaps pulling your child out of the regular education classroom for certain subjects would be better. For instance, during reading or math, she might go to the resource room where she can work with a teacher on the material that she doesn't understand. In which case, this would be your child's LRE.

But maybe this wouldn't work for her either. Maybe she is so far behind in reading that she would have great difficulty keeping up with the rest of the class in nearly all academic subjects. Remember, poor reading skills will not only affect reading or English class but also science, social studies, health, and math.

In this situation, maybe you want to your child to be in a special education classroom more or less all of the time, with the exception of nonacademic subjects such as art and physical education. That way, she can get the intensive academic support and remediation that she needs but also the social integration that she craves; in which case, this might be her LRE.

Finally, let's suppose that in addition to having a severe learning disability, your child has a number of behavior problems. Perhaps, she copes with her academic frustrations by getting into fights and being belligerent to her teachers. In this situation, being with her nondisabled students might be out of the question, even for nonacademic subjects. Not only would she be disrupting the entire class, but she wouldn't be learning anything either. Here you might decide that a self-contained classroom comprising nothing but other kids with special needs is most appropriate.

I could continue these examples forever. I could also suggest that your child is violent and dangerous to others and should be put in a psychiatric ward or a lockdown residential facility for juvenile delinquents. But hopefully you see what I am doing.

In this scenario, notice that I start with the "normal" environment—that is, regular education without any special supports. I then add supports and go to a slightly more contrived environment. I continue until I develop a situation where I can reasonably expect that the child would get an "appropriate education."

Furthermore, notice that I not only consider your child's needs but also the needs of her classmates and teachers. People often forget these aspects in determining an LRE. They only look at the child with disabilities and do not consider how that child's behavior might affect those around her. As a result, even if a child is physically integrated into a regular education environment, she might become socially isolated and ostracized.

WHAT IS AN IEP?

If you have been around special education at all, you have undoubtedly heard the letters *IEP*. Because the IEP is a cornerstone of special education, you better know something about it. Actually, you need to know a great deal about it!

Recall that *IEP* stands for *individualized education program*, which is a legally binding document that outlines what services, modifications, and support are going to be provided to your child. It also indicates what goals your child will be working on over the course of the year, such as improving his math abilities or social skills. In other words, as the *I* indicates, IEPs are *individually* constructed with your child's unique needs in mind.

IEPs are written by the IEP team, of which you should be part. Other members include your child's special education teacher, regular education teachers, and other school-related professionals. If you would like to include additional people on the IEP team, such as a family friend, lawyer, former teacher, and advocate, you are well within your rights to have them come along.

IEPs are good for 12 months and are usually written at the beginning of every school year. However, they can be written as often as needed. If things change, if you have a new idea to be put into an IEP, or if you are unhappy with the current IEP for any reason, you can call an IEP meeting at any time. When I was teaching, I had parents calling for IEP meetings every month. (But please don't do this without a reasonable cause!)

In summary, there are three main points that you need to understand about IEPs. The first is that they are important. They summarize what services and accommodations your child will be given at school. If you want your child to get some sort of modifications, accommodations, or services, make sure that it is written into the IEP.

Second, IEPs are legally binding. That means that if you and the school officials agree to services and have them listed in an IEP, then the school must provide those services. If the school doesn't follow through with what is written in an IEP, you can file for due process (which I talk about in a moment).

Finally, you are a vital member of the IEP team—and rightfully so. After all, you know your child better than anyone else. So, it is important that you actively participate in the creation of your child's IEP. In a little bit, I talk about how to do just that.

COMPONENTS OF IEPS

Writing about IEPs has become a bit problematic because the latest revision of IDEA has left many issues up to each state to decide. Specifically, a couple years ago, all IEPs were required to have what were called *short-term objectives*. These were statements of what steps students would take to achieve their ultimate goals for the year. For instance, if the student's goal was to improve reading, some short-term objectives might include the following:

"When presented with flash cards with third-grade reading words on them, Billy will say 85% of the words correctly."

"When instructed by his teacher, Billy will read a passage out loud with 95% accuracy."

"After reading an assigned story, Billy will answer 8 out of 10 comprehension questions correctly."

And so forth.

Short-term objectives are no longer required in IEPs by the federal government, but many states still require them. If you don't know where your state stands, ask your child's special education teacher or consult your state's department of education.

Although short-term objectives may or may not be in your child's IEPs, there are a few things that the federal government still requires, regardless of what state you live in. These include the following:

- present level of performance,
- annual goals,
- statement of services provided,
- LRE,
- accommodations for state and districtwide examinations,
- parental notification, and
- transition plan.

Present Level of Performance

According to IDEA, every IEP must have a thorough discussion of all recent and relevant data collected regarding your child. Think of this discussion as a snapshot of who your child is right when the IEP is being written. It will probably be found in a section referred to as the *PLOP* (present level of performance) or the *PLEP* (present level of educational performance). Regardless of what it is called, this section should contain everything that your child's teacher needs to know to teach your child effectively, including the following:

- results of recent standardized tests,
- behavioral observations,
- your child's strengths and interests,
- your child's primary learning style,
- your child's diagnosis, and
- an explanation as to how your child's disability affects his or her ability to progress in the general education curriculum.

Of course, you can add any other information that you believe is relevant. Again, the idea is to summarize your child so that teachers don't have to keep reinventing the wheel every year. So, if there are some strategies that work for your child or if there are reinforcers that are especially motivating, make sure that such information is put into the PLOP. That way, present and subsequent teachers will know about them.

Also, if there is information that you don't want in the PLOP, feel free to request that it be taken out. For instance, perhaps there are some overly negative comments about your child, or maybe you believe that some information is inaccurate; in either situation, you can have the information rewritten or taken out of the IEP altogether.

Annual Goals

Annual goals are measurable statements that outline what the IEP team believes the child should try to accomplish during the course of the year. For instance, the goals might focus on improving your child's ability to pay attention or socialize appropriately with peers, or they may focus on an increase in reading level or math ability, and so forth.

Now, just because something isn't listed in your child's annual goals doesn't mean that teachers won't cover it. In other words, you don't have to list absolutely everything that will be taught to your child over the course of the year. For example, even if the goals focus on paying attention, socializing, and reading ability, your child will still be taught history, science, and physical education.

Think of annual goals as that which will take priority during the coming school year. Other things that are part of the traditional curriculum will still be covered, but the issues addressed in the annual goals will receive particular attention.

Statement of Services Provided

IDEA also mandates that IEPs clearly list the services that will be provided to students. Moreover, IEPs must indicate when the services are going to start and what their expected frequency, duration, and location will be.

What services can be listed? Well, basically anything that your child needs to receive an appropriate education. Examples of services include the following:

- speech and language therapy,
- occupational therapy,
- physical therapy,

- classroom aides,
- tutors, and
- counseling.

If there is something that you want your child to have, make sure that it is indicated in the IEP. Also make sure that all agree on how frequently and how long these services are supposed to be given.

LRE

Somewhere within the IEP, there should be some indication of where your child will be taught. For example, there might be a chart or list (such as that illustrated in Table 11.4) that indicates where your child will be during each subject or class period.

Instead of a chart, there might simply be a narrative statement. For example, your child's IEP might say,

> Truman will be taught in the general education environment for all classes except for study hall and English, at which time he will receive special education services in the resource room.

Regardless of how the information is presented, you should know exactly where your child will be and when he or she will be in a regular education classroom or in a special education classroom. In many states, there has to be written justification why the child isn't fully included with your child's nondisabled peers.

Table 11.4. Sample Chart Indicating a Student's Schedule Within an Individualized Education Program

Period	Subject	Teacher	Location
1	English	Dr. Cimera	Resource Room
2	Science	Ms. Kroft	Room 313
3	Study Hall	Dr. Cimera	Resource Room
4	Lunch	—	Lunch Room
5	Physical Ed	Mr. Worester	West Gym
6	Social Studies	Mr. Jergen	Room 222
7	Art	Mr. Sutcliffe	Room 033

Accommodations for State and Districtwide Examinations

The fifth area that must be addressed in IEPs involves state and districtwide examinations. Most states and school districts require students to take certain tests at specific points in their education. For instance, in my school district, students had to take a reading test at 3rd grade, a general knowledge exam at 4th grade, a written expression exam at 5th grade, another general knowledge exam at 7th grade, a U.S. history exam at 8th grade, and a U.S. Constitution exam at 11th grade.

If your child needs any kind of modifications or accommodations for these tests, they must be listed somewhere in the IEP. Modifications and accommodations can include the following:

- having the tests read to your student;
- giving your student extra time to complete the tests;
- allowing frequent breaks during the tests;
- the use of calculators, dictionaries, or other support materials;
- taking the test in a quiet, isolated environment; and
- allowing your student to give oral responses to test question

Of course, you can request that your child not participate in any of these state or districtwide assessments. In these situations, the IEP would include an explanation why taking the tests would not be beneficial for your child.

Parental Notification

Given that parents are an integral part of the IEP team as well as their child's education, IDEA mandates that they be kept abreast of what is happening. Consequently, IEPs must have, in writing, an explanation regarding how parents will be informed about their child's progress. This explanation should include the method (e.g., via phone, mail, e-mail) and the frequency (e.g., once a week) that parents will be contacted.

Although there is no specific manner through which parents are contacted, IDEA does stipulate that parents of special education students be contacted at least as often as parents of nondisabled students are. For instance, if parents of regular education students in your child's school are contacted three times each semester, you must be contacted at least the same amount.

Of course, you can request being contacted more often. Many teachers whom I know send notes home with their students every day. Although I find this effort commendable, I wonder how long my colleagues can keep up such communication. After all, they probably have an average of 20 to 25 kids. That is a lot of note writing every day!

I suppose that what I am hinting at is this: I realize that you may want a great deal of contact with your child's teachers. But please keep in mind that they have many other students. Moreover, their jobs tend to be pretty stressful, and they tend to guard what little free time that they have. If a teacher prefers to contact you once a week, maybe that is more appropriate than every day or every other day. Then again, it all depends on your given situation.

Transition Plan

Finally, IDEA mandates that IEPs must plan for the student's eventual transition to postsecondary school life. Specifically, by age 14, your child's IEP must begin addressing transition issues, such as teaching skills that are required for adult life. By age 16, IEPs must include interagency linkages that will help your child transition to adulthood. For example, a representative from the local community college, state university, or department of vocational rehabilitation might be invited to attend the IEP meeting to discuss postschool programs appropriate for your child.

Notice that I said *by* age 14 and *by* age 16. Actually, IDEA says *by* these dates or *as needed*. So you can certainly begin addressing transition issues well before these times. For instance, I personally believe that every IEP, regardless of the child's age, should prepare the student for adulthood. I mean, if a goal or service isn't going to help the child in the future, then why is it in the IEP?

Finally, a year before your child reaches the age of majority, he will need to be notified of his rights. Once your child turns 18 years old, he will be his own guardian and will have the legal authority to make his own decisions.

PARTICIPATING IN YOUR CHILD'S IEP

It would be easy for me to tell you what IEPs are and then say, "Now, help create them." But that really wouldn't be very constructive. What I want to do now is give you some practical advice for when you work with special education teachers and other IEP members, myself included. We are, I must admit, a strange breed.

Save and Document Everything

My first suggestion is to make sure that you have copies of all important forms, letters, reports, and other documents. I strongly suggest that you get a file cabinet. By the time that your child graduates from high school, you are going to have a mountain of paperwork. If you can't decide what is important and what is not, save it all. Save every little note that is sent home. Save progress reports. Save everything!

I also highly recommend that you communicate with your child's teachers in writing. I don't want that to sound paranoid or anything. I don't mean it that way. It is just that mistakes happen and memories fade. Moreover, as a teacher, I had 30 kids to think about. I frequently forgot what I told whom. Having things in writing helped me.

Moreover, with the advent of the Internet and e-mail, it is easy to get a hold of someone, and it is easy for that person to reply when the chance presents itself. If you were to call me at work, I would have a million and one things going on. I may or may not be able to answer your question or even talk with you. But if you e-mail me, I can think about my reply and get back to you when I can. Plus, with e-mail, both parties have a copy of what has been said. Personally, I think e-mail is a godsend.

Be Prepared

Okay, so you have a big stack of dead trees neatly organized in a giant eight-drawer filing cabinet. Now what?

Well, I hate to sound like a Boy Scout, but my next piece of advice is "be prepared." Without your being prepared, the IEP meeting will most likely be a waste of time. You need to be ready before the meeting actually starts. How do you do this?

First of all, before you have any meetings with your child's teachers, review what the last meeting was about. You should have been given an agenda as well as minutes, which summarize what was said in the meeting. These are good reminders of what had happened. At the very least, keep organized notes yourself.

After you review your notes and minutes, brainstorm a list of questions, suggestions, or random thoughts; just write down whatever comes to mind. Then prioritize anything that you want to discuss. This will help you make sure that you cover the important things first.

See Other Perspectives

Being a teacher isn't easy (neither is being a parent, of course; or even a kid, for that matter). Your biggest concern is your child. The teacher's biggest concern is your child and several dozen more.

I know that teachers might seem a bit stuck on themselves from time to time, present company included. We tend to say things like "I'm changing the world one child at a time" and "Those who can, teach." We sometimes forget that there are other professions out there who do just as much, if not more, for the world as we do.

But teaching is a thankless job. Moreover, it is a very difficult job. Yes, we get our summers off, but we usually spend that time preparing for the next school year. Plus, we don't get paid that much. When I started teaching in the late-1980s, I earned about $14,000. That's not exactly a windfall! By and large, most teachers are in the field because they want to make a difference in a child's life. So if we ever express an opinion different from yours, just keep in mind that we are all on the same team. We all want to help your child.

Consider what your child's teachers have to say. Think about their perspectives and then judge their ideas and comments with a positive point of view. Remember, we aren't trying to make you upset or harm your child. We really are trying to help.

Stick by Your Guns

Going to IEP meetings can be intimidating. You will probably be surrounded by all of the professionals, with fancy titles and degrees, talking in a kind of code (IEPs, PLOPs, etc.). But you are there to advocate for your kid, and you know more about your child than anyone with a doctorate does. So, if you have an idea or if you think that what the school officials are proposing is wrong, then tell them.

If they try to change your mind, well . . . listen to them. But don't be pushed aside or minimized. Your viewpoint has just as much merit, if not more, than theirs. Stick by your guns. Keep saying no or whatever it is that you want to say.

If you feel too intimidated to take a stand, then get an advocate to help you. There are many professional organizations for family members who have kids in special education. The resources section in the back of the book lists many of them that focus on learning disabilities. Contact them and see if they have a chapter in your state.

Alternately, at the very least, bring a friend to the meetings. There is comfort in numbers. Plus, that person might be able to give you a neutral perspective.

Be Gracious

As I have said before, being a teacher is a thankless job. None of my students ever comes up to me and says, "Gee, Dr. Cimera, you really made me work hard, and I learned a lot. Thank you." So when you get the opportunity to work with really good teachers, let them know that you appreciate their effort.

I am not saying that you should go out and buy each of your child's teachers a Mercedes or anything like that, nor am I implying that teachers will only do a good job for your kid if you buy them things. I am just suggesting that if you value something that a teacher, principal, counselor, or whoever did, then show it. Send a card with the words *Thank you. I really appreciate everything that you do*. Or even a quick e-mail or a handwritten note on a dirty napkin. Believe me, teachers are starved for attention and praise. A little kindness goes a long way.

WHAT SHOULD YOU DO IF YOU DISAGREE WITH SCHOOL PERSONNEL?

In this chapter, I have been talking about your rights as a parent of a student in special education. I hope that you understand that you are part of a team that will be working hard to give your child the skills and services that he or she needs to succeed in life.

But what if you don't agree with the other IEP team members or school personnel? The first thing to do is to try to work things out. Present your position as clearly and objectively as possible. Also, listen to what everyone has to say. Maybe some of the team members have valid points. Furthermore, as strained as your conversations might get, try to remember that teachers are teachers because they love kids and want the best for your child, too.

However, when you and the school simply cannot come to an agreement, one thing that you can do is take the school to due process. Basically, what this means is that you file a complaint with your state's department of education and ask for a third party to come in to solve the impasse. The state will appoint an independent third-party person to hear both sides and then make a ruling.

Now, I have been on both sides of the table during due process hearings. I have testified for parents, and I have testified for schools. And in most cases, I found the whole affair to be exceedingly stressful.

It is very much like being in a courtroom. One side calls various witnesses and makes its arguments. Then the other side gets to cross-examine the witnesses. And then they switch. The second side calls its witnesses, whom the first side gets to cross-examine as well. Eventually, the hearing officer makes a ruling.

I would like to make two important recommendations for when you ever have a conflict with a school. First, realize that even if you win an arbitration, you still have to deal with the personnel at your child's school. Don't be a poor winner. In fact, you should make an honest attempt to smooth things over and rebuild your relationship.

Second and most important, get an advocate who knows special education law. The school will have lawyers who do this for a living. You need someone on your side, if only to give you emotional support.

If you don't have an advocate who can go with you to meetings or help you frame your arguments, check out some of the websites and support groups presented in the back of the book. Many of the organizations and support groups have links to people in your state or region. They might be able to help you find someone who can help you.

You can even hire a lawyer. There are many lawyers who specialize in disability or education law. If you do go this route, make sure that you check the person out before you sign anything. Check to make sure that the person has a license and is familiar with your state's laws.

OTHER LEGALITIES

As I say at the beginning of this chapter, the legalities of special education can fill many books. I have covered many of the key points in brief detail. Now, before we end for good, I want to talk about some of the other legal issues that might be of interest to you. As always, if you need additional information, please consult the resources in the back of this text or speak to a lawyer specializing in such matters.

Access to Information

One of the other legalities that you should know about involves access to information. You are entitled to see anything that has your child's name on it. Anything. Even if a teacher keeps a journal about what happened in class, even if it is her or his own private thoughts, if she or he talks about your child, you are supposed to have access to that information.

Management of Your Child's File

Your child's schools will undoubtedly keep several files on your student. There will be the main file, which should be kept under lock and key in the front or special education office. This will have copies of your student's past and present IEPs, assessment reports, letters to and from you, and all other official information. There will also probably be a working file, which your child's special education teacher keeps in his or her office. This contains data on how your child is progressing on various goals, as well as observational notes and daily issues such as attendance.

Legally, you have access to these and any other files. Moreover, you have some control over what is in them. For example, let's suppose that the school psychologist does an assessment on your daughter and you disagree with the conclusions. The report says that your child has mental retardation, and you don't concur. Perhaps, you believe that your daughter was just having a bad day when she took the test. Or maybe she didn't try.

At any rate, you can request that that information be removed from the file so that no one else sees it. If the school declines to take the apparently erroneous information out of the file, you can take them through due process, and a hearing officer can decide if the information warrants staying.

Confidentiality

Confidentiality is usually taken pretty seriously in special education. I am not saying that it is always followed, for good and bad reasons, but it is something that is always talked about. At one school in which I worked, there were little posters in the office of Uncle Sam pointing his finger at the reader with the words "Does Everyone Need to Know That?"

Theoretically, you can limit who has access to what information. Not everyone needs to know private information about your child, including your child's diagnosis, past history, and so forth. Technically speaking, people aren't even supposed to know that your child is in special education unless you say it is okay for them to know. Of course, some things are pretty easy to figure out without anybody saying as much.

For school personnel to share information about your child, you will need to sign a consent form. The consent form must clearly contain the following details:

- what information is going to be shared,
- who has access to that information,
- for what purpose the information can be used, and
- a date at which the consent form expires.

It is important to note that you can withdraw your consent at any time. Moreover, consent forms usually only last the school year, so you may be asked to sign a new one every September.

If you have any concerns or wish that certain information be limited to certain people, feel free to voice your concerns to the special education teacher or the school's principal. Not everyone is entitled to all information about your child.

What information might you want to restrict? Well, that is up to you. I taught at a school where I was not allowed to review my own students' files for the first couple weeks of the school year. The idea was that past reports would bias my opinion of the child, which I personally believe to be true. If I am told that a kid has ADHD, every time he fidgets or looks around, I would be apt to say, "Ah! There it is. Of course, he has ADHD." I think that people are very susceptible to suggestion and have difficulty looking at children objectively. As such, maybe you would prefer not to notify the regular educators of your child's disability. That is common.

Alternately, maybe there is information that is too personal to be shared. For instance, one of our former foster daughters (let's call her Tiffany) had a traumatic childhood. She was repeatedly sexually assaulted by her father and his male friends. This information was in Tiffany's file but was later removed because her mother didn't want anybody to know—and rightfully so. It is no one's business.

However, please be cognizant that some personal information may be needed for teachers to be effective. For example, in the case of my foster daughter, she had a male teacher who (according to Tiffany) kept looking at her "funny." Furthermore, the teacher would pat her on the back, which made Tiffany scream and run out of the room. She simply felt uncomfortable around men and couldn't be touched by them.

Tiffany's special education teacher knew about Tiffany's childhood, so she understood why Tiffany was acting the way that she was. However, the special education teacher was not at liberty to say to the regular education teacher, "Hey, Tiff has had a really rough time with men. Be very careful not to touch her or make comments about her clothes or whatever." Maybe the regular education teacher should have been told, maybe not. You'll have to decide for yourself.

Manifest Determination and Discipline

Disciplining kids with disabilities is a touchy subject. I mean, think about it. Suppose that you are a regular education teacher trying to get through a lesson so that you can go home, relax, and watch an episode of *CSI* in peace and quiet. But you can't teach effectively, because students get up on their chairs and yell, "I am a rabbit. And some day we will ALL BE RABBITS . . . " Then they then hop around the classroom in a bunny line. (That actually happened in my class, by the way.)

Or imagine that you were repeatedly physically assaulted by a student. (This has happened to me as well.) Or imagine that someone called you filthy names nearly every day. (This has also happened to me.) Or whatever.

Wouldn't you be frustrated? Wouldn't you eventually get burnt out and want to leave your chosen profession? Wouldn't you want to discipline the children who were being disruptive, hostile, or just silly?

But wait a minute. What if these students had a disability that was causing or at least contributing to their inappropriate behavior? For instance, my student who was a rabbit had mental retardation. There wasn't a day that went by when he didn't announce his "rabbitdom." The student who hit, kicked, and bit me had autism. The student who kept calling me filthy names . . . well, he was just a very angry boy with several behavior disorders. Honestly, if I had his life, I would be cussing up a storm, too!

Should children be punished for things that are the result of their disabilities, especially if they can't control themselves? IDEA and the courts have said no. A child cannot be punished for something that is the result of a disability—unless the parents agree or the discipline plan (often called a *behavior intervention plan*) is written as part of the child's IEP.

Now, admittedly, this rule applies more to kids with mental retardation and behavior disorders than it does to kids with learning disabilities. After all, the fact that your child has difficulty reading, doing math, or expressing herself probably isn't going to result in any uncontrollable behavior. Still, you might be interested in this topic.

The process is called *manifestation determination*, and it goes something like this. For the sake of simplicity, let's suppose that your child has mental retardation and, one day, brought a gun to school. Of course, he didn't realize it was a real gun, and he didn't know that he could get into trouble for bringing it to class. If your child were a regular education student, he would be expelled. There would probably be few questions asked. He might even be charged with a crime. However, because he is a special education student, he can't just be kicked out of school, at least not permanently. He can only be removed temporarily while the IEP team decides whether the behavior was the result of his disability. If the IEP team determines that the behavior was stemming from the disability, the student can't be expelled. However, if the behavior wasn't caused by the disability, then he can be punished as any other child would be, including being expelled.

Taking Your Kid out of Special Education

This little tidbit is probably going to surprise you. Once your child is enrolled in special education, you can't just pull her out unilaterally. You can't say, "I don't want my child to be in special education any longer. I want her to be a regular education student." Well, yes, you can say that, but it doesn't mean that it will happen.

You see, leaving special education is considered a change in one's LRE. Before a student's LRE can be changed, the IEP team has to agree. Technically, if you want your child out of special education and if the rest of the IEP team doesn't agree, then your child stays in special education.

I know parents who actually moved out of a school district because they didn't want their son in special education anymore, but the rest of the IEP team disagreed. The family took the school to due process. The due process hearing officer concurred with the school and said that the child still needed special education services. So, the family moved.

However, don't get me wrong. Children graduate out of special education all of the time. For instance, let's suppose that your child is enrolled in special education because a learning disability adversely affects her ability to get an appropriate education. After 3 years, she is reevaluated, and the evaluation team concludes that the learning disability no longer affects her as severely as it once did. Perhaps, she has been taught ways to learn more efficiently and is now excelling. In such case, she would no longer be entitled to special education services, because she doesn't have a disability that adversely affects her ability to obtain an appropriate education.

Notification of Your Rights

Finally, every year, you should be notified of your rights in writing. This will probably be done at your child's IEP meeting, or the school will send you a pamphlet or guidebook at the beginning of every school year. Regardless of when you receive your statement of rights, make sure that you keep it handy. File it away with your child's past IEPs, assessments, report cards, and the reams of other paperwork that you will be getting throughout the years.

SUMMARY

If your child has a learning disability, he or she could be eligible for special education. In this chapter, I talk about what special education is and what your rights are as a parent. As I say at the beginning, the legal aspects of special education can fill several books, so I cover only basic information in general detail. If you would like a more in-depth discussion of legal topics, please consult the resources listed in the back, or consult a lawyer.

12

LEARNING DISABILITIES AND ADULTHOOD

Well, here we are at the final chapter. I hope that you have learned something useful about learning disabilities, not only what they are, but how to help people with specific kinds of learning disabilities. Before we leave each other's company, there are a few last things that I need to cover. Specifically, I need to talk about how to prepare a child with a learning disability for life as an adult. That, after all, is the goal of parenting and teaching, isn't it? I want to take these remaining pages and get you to think about various aspects of adult life for people who have learning disabilities.

HIGH SCHOOL VOCATIONAL TRAINING PROGRAMS

I want begin our last discussion by discussing the various secondary education programs that are often available to high school students with learning disabilities. Personally, I think that this topic is underdiscussed. Unfortunately, no one seems to ever mention the options that are available to kids with disabilities. It is as if everyone thinks that children have to be in the regular education classroom 100% of the time if they are going to be successful in life, and this simply isn't true.

As a student, I was fully included in regular education. I had some speech services when I was in elementary school, but other than that, I was just a normal student who happened to have a learning disability. Even though everything turned out okay and I was able to get into college and earn a doctorate, I think that I would have done better had I had another option like today's kids do.

In the end, you have to decide where your child should be taught. But please don't forget about some alternative programs just because you think that all children should go to their local schools and attend regular education classes. Although that might be great for some children with learning disabilities, maybe your child would be better off in some of the other programs that are now available.

School-Based Vocational Programs

With the growing push to prepare kids with disabilities for their vocational future, many schools are offering in-house vocational programs designed to teach students the skills that they will need in order to obtain and maintain employment. These programs have curriculums that teach students marketable skills—anything from computer programming to automotive repair. They also teach students how to find jobs, fill out applications, complete resumes, and interview. Many also teach the social skills required for working with other people.

These programs are taught in the regular school for usually one or two periods a day. So basically, while other students are in homeroom or study hall, kids with learning and other disabilities go to another room, where they learn vocational skills.

Community-Based High School Program

Some schools have vocational programs in the community. This is what I used to teach when I taught high school students. You see, my school would have five or six employers who were willing to hire our students on a temporary basis. My students would then sample a different type of job every couple of months. For instance, a student might work at a bank doing clerical or computer work. Then the following month he would work at a preschool, helping teach little kids. Then maybe he would go to a country club or golf course, where he would do landscape maintenance. And so forth.

Typically, my students went to school for the first half of the day to attend their academic classes. Right before lunch, they went to their jobs for 3 or 4 hours. I trained and supervised them as they needed, but generally speaking, they were in the hands of their employers. The idea was to give students experiences in a range of potential jobs. This helped them decide what they wanted to do (and didn't want to do) with their lives.

The vocational experiences also taught my students valuable skills that they couldn't learn in the classroom, such as conflict resolution, problem solving, and a strong work ethic. Okay, yes . . . some of these skills can be taught in the classroom, but my students seemed to learn them better and quicker when they were actually doing meaningful work in the community. Plus, they were highly motivated by getting a paycheck.

I want to point out that if your child's school doesn't have a school- or community-based vocational program already set up, your child can still gain such experiences. All you have to do is have your child's IEP reflect your wishes to have an in-school or community-based vocational program. Even if the school doesn't have an existing curriculum, if the IEP indicates that your child will get various vocational experiences, then the school has to develop the curriculum.

Vocational High Schools

In addition to vocational programs through the regular public schools, there are also special high schools that focus exclusively on learning valuable trades. For example, one of our local vocational schools has programs where students learn the skills needed to become automotive mechanics, carpenters, electricians, health care workers, and many other professionals. Students enrolled in these schools are still taught academics, such as reading, writing, and arithmetic. But these lessons are worked into the field of study that the students have chosen to pursue. Everything is applied.

I can't say enough positive things about these schools. The ones that I have visited teach their students valuable skills in creative, hands-on ways. Furthermore, they often have job placement programs where students graduate with full-time positions. Many of these positions pay more than what I make as a university professor.

There are usually long waiting lists for these kinds of vocational programs. So, if this interests you or your child, I suggest that you look into them as soon as possible.

Charter Schools

Another trend in education is the proliferation of charter schools. Charter schools are alternative schools typically funded by private and public money. They are often geared toward certain types of student. For example, a charter school down the road is designed for students who are at risk of dropping out of school. Another one is for gifted and talented students. Others are for kids who have learning disabilities.

Charter schools usually offer smaller class sizes than do regular public schools. Furthermore, they often have newer facilities that include up-to-date technology. However, the traditional selling point of charter schools is that, given the smaller class sizes, their faculties are able to use more hands-on and small group activities.

To locate charter schools in your area, talk with your local school officials or access your state's board of education website. However, before you attempt to sign your child up, realize that these programs frequently have long waiting lists. Moreover, not all charter schools are exceptional. Several have been closed for inappropriate educational practices.

Before you elect to send your child to a charter school, check it out first. Take a tour of the facilities. Talk with the teachers and administrators, and ask other parents if they have heard anything, good or bad, about the school's programs.

GETTING INTO COLLEGE

Whenever I give workshops on learning disabilities and begin talking about college, many parents and teachers immediately raise their hands and say, "Our children can barely pass high school. How can they be expected to get into college?"

There are a number of comments that I make to them. The first is that their attitude isn't helpful. It is immensely demoralizing to have your parents or teachers say something to the effect of "Well, I doubt that you can get accepted into college." Why should your child even bother to try if you don't think that he or she will succeed?

I know that probably sounds like an insignificant comment to you, but children really do live up (or down) to the expectations of their teachers and parents—it's the self-fulfilling prophecy. If you imply that they won't get into college, they probably won't. So try to be positive.

Moreover, you should realize that study after study has shown that academic success in high school does not correlate strongly with academic success in college. College and high school are completely different and require different skills. For example, in high school, you have sit in a chair all day and take a lot of classes that you aren't interested in. You may have a few electives here and there, but generally speaking, you have to take whatever the school requires. Furthermore, high school classes tend to rely heavily on rote memorization.

In college, you select different areas of focus. You can be a history major or go into marketing, English, political science, whatever. Yes, you might have to take English 101 or a certain number of math classes to graduate, but by and large, you get to select most of your classes. Furthermore, you don't have classes all day. You may have a class that meets for an hour every Monday, Wednesday, and Friday or one that meets for an hour and a half every Tuesday and Wednesday. But you won't have to be sitting on your butt, listening to some teacher from 8:00 to 3:00. This makes the time that you spend in class far more tolerable, if not enjoyable.

Finally, college courses tend to be product driven. You have to produce something in most courses, whether it is a report, speech, or project. And although there are still exams, they tend to focus less on rote memorization of facts and more on high-level questions, such as those requiring divergent thinking.

The second comment that I make to parents and teachers who doubt their children's ability to get into college is this: "Do you know how easy it is to get into college these days?" I don't mean to sound flippant or disparaging, but most students can get into a public college nowadays. They might not get into Harvard or Princeton, but they will probably get into your local state college. At the very least, they will probably get in on academic probation, which means that they have to pass their classes to stay in school.

Now, I am not saying that your child will get into her program of choice. For example, even though I was toward the bottom of my high school class and did poorly on my SAT, I was able to get into Purdue University. However, I wouldn't have been able to get into its nuclear engineering program. It has high standards and is extremely competitive. Only the best of the best get in. Still, even with my poor performance in high school, I was able to get in and (with help) graduate from college.

The question that most parents and teachers seem to have is "How do we get our students into college? What about the SAT and all of that stuff?" Let's take a few minutes and talk about some of these issues.

Taking the SAT, ACT, and Other Entrance Exams

The first thing that your child has to do to get into most colleges is take the SAT, ACT, or some other standardized test. Which one your child has to take depends on the school. I have always heard that the ACT is easier, but I am sure that it depends on personal preference.

So, the first thing that your child needs to do is find out what tests are required. You can usually find this information on the application material provided by the colleges. The next thing that your child should do is sign up for any and all study classes or seminars that are available for that particular test. They are well worth the registration fees. Most such classes furnish valuable test-taking tips, such as whether or not to guess. They also frequently offer sample exams on which your child can practice. Also have your child check out books about the test. There are tons of resource books and study guides on the SAT and ACT. I cite a few in the resource list.

Of course, once your child gets all of these resources, he needs to practice—and practicing doesn't mean reading and rereading the material. It means having someone quiz him and ask him questions. It means sitting down with a sample exam and pretending that he is taking it for real.

Furthermore, you might want to consider having some IEP goals developed involving test preparation. For instance, maybe your child's special education teacher could spend a half an hour a week going over sample questions with your child. Many special education programs even have study groups or clubs where students get together and practice for the SAT and ACT.

The next step is to find out when the tests are administered. I highly recommend that your child take the tests as soon as possible. This will give him an opportunity to retake the test should he need to. As a matter of fact, maybe your child should go into the first test with the mind-set of "This doesn't count. I am just practicing." This might take some of the pressure off, and as a consequence, he might do better than expected.

Something else to consider is accommodations. For example, maybe your child has a learning disability in reading and needs extra time to read passages. Such modifications can be arranged with the testing centers; however, they must be notified before your child takes the test. If your child walks in moments before the test is about to begin and requests various accommodations, he will probably be denied.

Yet another consideration is how the test should be taken. You see, many testing centers allow students to take tests on computer. They sit in front of computer screens and answer questions that appear before them. I did this when I took the GRE (to get into graduate school), and personally, I don't recommend it. I found it difficult to read from a computer screen for an extended period (remember, these tests take a couple hours). Moreover, the computer wouldn't let me go back and check or change my answers to previously viewed questions, which I didn't know at the time. I missed a lot of points from questions that I left blank thinking that I could answer them later.

Finally, your child should get a good night's sleep before the test and show up early. Above all, he needs to go to the bathroom right before the test! A friend of mine was drinking a bottle of water right before the test started. Halfway before the exam ended, he had to pee and pee badly. Unfortunately, the test administrator would not let him out of the testing room. After several very uncomfortable yet funny moments (funny to me, at least), my friend just got up and ran out of the room. His results were nullified, and he had to retake the exam.

Finding the Right School

Something else that you and your child need to consider is finding the right school. A number of factors come into play depending on your situation. First and foremost is cost. How much do you want to spend?

There is also the right location. Out-of-state schools are typically more expensive than in-state schools. Furthermore, although your child might love to go to a university three blocks away from a beach, you have to ask yourself, is that going to be the proper educational environment? Maybe, if your child wants to be a marine biologist.

Your child also has to consider the degrees and programs that the school offers. If your child wants to be a nurse or a doctor, make sure that the schools to which she applies has good programs in those areas. How do you determine if the programs are good? You can talk with the faculty of the programs, but in all honesty, they aren't going to tell you, "You know, we really don't have a good program. Try going to some other university." Instead, go to your public library. There are tons of books that rank colleges on their costs, academics, sports teams, and even the quality of their parties. I am serious. The University of Wisconsin at Madison is continually rated as the best party school in the nation. Go Badgers!

As you and your child are researching potential schools, don't forget to see if they have special services for students with disabilities. All universities that get federal and state funding have to have some services, such as wheelchair-accessible bathrooms and classrooms. However, many universities have programs to help students with learning disabilities. For instance, my school has a great program called Project Success. It helps students learn how to study effectively. It gives them mentors, who give support to new students. The program also allows students to get help on their homework.

Check out your child's potential schools. See if they have programs that help students with learning disabilities. A little help can mean the difference between graduating with honors and dropping out.

Finally, find out whether the faculty members are accessible and friendly. Walk around the campus and go into the buildings. Are many professors in their offices? Ask them questions. Are they willing to spend a couple minutes with you? You don't want to have your child go to any university where he or she can't talk with his or her teachers.

Finding the Right Field of Study

Most students enter college without a clear idea of what they want to do. I am middle-aged, and I am still trying to figure out what I want to do when I grow up! Don't get too worried if your child is on the fence about what career she wants to enter after school. Still, your child is eventually going to have to select a major. What should she do if she can't decide?

The first thing that I suggest is that your child sample different classes and professions. It is perfectly acceptable for students to audit courses; that is, they sit in on the classes but aren't actually enrolled in them. They don't take the tests or get a grade. They just observe. Furthermore, encourage your child to use his summers to get internships or part-time jobs at various companies or in diverse fields. He will never really know if he likes a particular profession until he sees it up close and personal.

I also recommend that your child speak with guidance counselors at the university. Guidance counselors know a great deal about many areas of study. Furthermore, they have vocational interest inventories that help people decide what they might be good at.

Emotional Support

I recently read an article on why students leave college before they graduate. What do you think the number one reason is? It isn't that the work is too hard. That is way down on the list. Students who struggle with the academics usually just change fields of study to something that better matches their skills. Nor is the number one reason for early departure financial. That is the second-most-common reason.

The number one reason why students drop out of college is that they were lonely. Some missed their high school friends. Others had boyfriends or girlfriends who went to different schools. A few even missed their parents.

The implications are pretty clear. To enhance your child's chances of succeeding at college, you have to encourage him or her to develop healthy emotional supports. Notice that I say *healthy*. I know a lot of college students who end up going out every night and getting drunk or stoned and forget why they are in school.

For kids with disabilities, healthy relationships are critical. It seems that many kids with learning disabilities go wild when they are no longer under the watchful eyes of parents and teachers.

So, how can your child get the emotional support that she needs? One is to become active in the school community. She can join clubs, sports, or any of the hundreds of organizations that are common on college campuses.

I strongly suggest that your child join organizations for nontraditional students or students with disabilities. By being with other students who have learning difficulties, your child can feel less alone. Furthermore, he can gain valuable knowledge, such as which professors are the most accommodating, which classes should be taken at what time, and where to go for help.

POSTSECONDARY EDUCATION OPTIONS

When I talk about having students with learning disabilities continue their education after high school, many people only think about 4-year colleges or universities. But there are so many other options that are out there. Here are just a few.

Community College

If I had my life to do over again, I wouldn't have gone to a 4-year university right after high school. I think that I would have instead gone to a community college, at least for the first year.

I wasn't ready for the social and academic demands of a big university such as Purdue. My first semester, I started drinking and partying, and because none of my professors cared whether I attended class or not, I often skipped.

Community colleges not only cost less than 4-year universities but also tend to have small class sizes and more one-on-one help from the instructors. Consequently, such schools might be a good match for your child. The only suggestion that I have is to make sure that the courses taken at the community college can be transferred to other universities. Sometimes, students go to a community college with the notion of transferring to a larger university later on. However, not all classes transfer. So, in the end, they have to retake them.

Tech and Trade Schools

Tech and trade schools focus on preparing students for specific careers, such as nursing assistants, computer programmers, and so forth. Much like community colleges, tech and trade schools tend to have small class sizes and extra one-on-one help from instructors. They also have considerable hands-on teaching.

Universities

As I said, I went to a 4-year university. For me, it worked out fine. Universities tend to offer far more fields of study and academic resources than do other postsecondary educational options. Moreover, you can't reach some goals, such as becoming a doctor or a lawyer, without a university degree.

However, some universities have some downsides. They are often much bigger than community colleges, thereby making it easy for students to feel as if they are just numbers and not people. I teach over a hundred students a semester. I simply can't know all of them by name.

SKILLS FOR SUCCESS IN POSTSECONDARY EDUCATION

Regardless of where your child ends up continuing her education or even if she goes straight from high school to work, there are several key skills that she will need to be successful. In this section, I want to talk about some of these. However, I want to stress the importance of formal instruction regarding this issue. I strongly recommend that she take a study skills course. Most high schools and colleges have one.

Active Learning

The problem that I see with most of my students, with and without disabilities, is that they don't know how to study. It is hard to explain, but it is as if my students just listen or read information and then expect to be able to recall it. Moreover, they are only interested in remembering information, not processing or applying it.

I have talked about this a little bit before, but for people to really learn something, they have to actively think about it. For instance, you can't just look at these words and expect to get anything out of them. You have to think about the meaning behind them. You then have to apply the meaning to your life. When you are reading about characteristics of various learning disabilities, you should be thinking about what is being discussed and apply it to your child's situation. Don't just let the words echo around in your head. Think about them. Summarize them in your own words. Give them meaning beyond what they actually say.

Reading

It also surprises me that many of my college students don't know how to read a textbook. You see, they approach it as if they are reading a novel, which is wrong. Let me explain.

When you read a novel or something interesting, you read each and every word. You start at the beginning of the first chapter and keep reading until you reach the end of the last chapter. Students shouldn't do this when reading a textbook for a class. They should begin by surveying the chapter. They should look at the title of the chapter and all of the headings. They should look at the pictures and read the captions. From this information, they should formulate questions regarding the main themes of the chapter:

- What is the chapter about?
- What terms keep reappearing?
- What will I have to remember after reading the chapter?

Once your child has skimmed the chapter and has asked herself some cursory questions, she should thoroughly read the summary or conclusion at the end of the chapter. If there are chapter questions or a case study at the beginning of the chapter, she should read that as well. Finally, your child should skim the rest of the chapter, paying particular attention to anything in bold or italics. She shouldn't read each word of every sentence. Instead, she should pick out the main topic sentences of each paragraph. If there is a concept that she doesn't understand, then she should read that section more comprehensively.

As your child surveys, skims, and reads the chapter, the questions that she asked herself (e.g., "What is the main theme?") should be answered. Again, the idea here is to actively read rather than just let the words go through one's head.

Note Taking in Class

Note taking is an art. Unfortunately, no one seems to teach students how to do it. For instance, most of my students write exactly what I have said or put on the board. Your child shouldn't do this. First of all, little of what I say as a teacher is really important. Second, when students spend all of their energies writing what I have said or put up on over-heads, they are unable to think about what is being discussed.

Effective note takers are able to find the key points of the lecture and then write them down quickly without losing the flow of the discussion. Now, I am not suggesting that all students need to learn to write in shorthand, although it certainly couldn't hurt. What I am suggesting is that rather than write down everything, students should identify major themes and then write them down with brief explanations.

Moreover, students should write things down in their own words, unless they are trying to remember a direct quote or something that they need to remember verbatim. By putting things into their own words, students have to think about the meaning of what is presented to them. They then have to reformulate the meaning into something that they can better understand. Not only does writing things down in their own words help students to process information more deeply, but it also helps students recall the information from their memories better. After all, it is easier to recall something that you said rather than what someone else said.

Of course, for students, the most critical aspect of taking notes is writing so that they can understand what the notes mean months later. They should write as neatly as possible, without taking too much time. Furthermore, they should include enough detail so that they can remember what everything means but not so much that they fall behind the teacher and miss content.

Finally, students should never use abbreviations unless they can remember what the abbreviations mean months later. For example, writing *USA* is fine. However, if they are going to write *SLD* for *specific learning disabilities* (and they are new to this term), they should write the definition of the abbreviation (e.g., "SLD = specific learning disability") at the top of the page or somewhere noticeable.

Here is a summary of how to take notes:

- Write only key ideas or what needs to be remembered.
- Write in your own words, unless exact quotes need to be recalled.
- Use bullets or phrases when appropriate.
- Don't use abbreviations, unless they are common or defined in the notes.
- Write neatly.

Highlighting Textbooks

Have you ever looked at some of the used textbooks sold at bookstores? Some of them look as if they have fallen into a bucket of paint or have been highlighted with a large roller! You can tell right away that the previous owner of the book probably didn't get a lot out of it.

Highlighting books is much like taking notes from lectures. First, you want to highlight only what matters. If you highlight more than a half the page, you have highlighted way too much. Moreover, try to use only one color of highlighter, especially if you are using a used text that already has some highlighting in it. If you use more than one, you might get confused about which are your highlights and which are the previous owner's markings. When you come to a long section that has a great deal of relevant information, rather than highlight everything, put a big star or a line next to it. This will call your attention to this passage when it is time to study.

In addition to just highlighting, jot down notes in the margins of the text. You can make notes particularly effective if you tie them to what was discussed in class or in the text. In summary,

- Highlight only what matters.
- Use only one color of highlighter.
- Rather than highlight an entire section or table, put a star by it.
- Jot down notes in the margins to help you remember key information.

Organization

Organization is another key to surviving college (and life in general). Imagine that you spend an entire weekend writing a stellar paper, but right as you are about to turn it in, you can't find it. This happens to my students with startling regularity. And when they come to me all upset and teary eyed, begging for an extension, I have to point to the syllabus and remind them that there is a 15% penalty for late homework.

Being organized is a bit of an art, and your child will have to find the system that will work best for her. For example, I am a sticky-note kind of guy. Anything that I need to remember goes on a yellow note that gets stuck along the edge of my computer monitor. My wife, however, is a PDA person. She has one of those little handheld computer thingies that keeps track of all of her appointments and information. She has every name, phone number, birth date, and anniversary that she will ever need entered into it. It even beeps a half an hour before she has a meeting. Other people like date books. Still, others have complete filing systems with tabs and expandable folders and so forth. What your child uses depends on her needs. However, I have a few suggestions to make.

First, the organization system should be manageable. That is, it should keep track of everything that is important (e.g., assignments and due dates), without consuming a great deal of time. Second, your child will have to use the same system consistently. It does no good to write some things on sticky notes and then others in a notebook and still others in a PDA. Too much time would get wasted looking for things. Plus, information is likely to get lost. So encourage your child to use one system habitually.

Finally, suppose that your child develops a great system for keeping track of things. He has his English stuff in a green folder, his science in a blue folder, social studies in a red folder, and so on. He even writes in a day planner everything that he needs to do. How effective is this system going to be if he never checks his day planner when he needs to or has the correct folders when he needs them?

I learned this the hard way. I would write down appointments on sticky notes, but I would forget to look at them. Consequently, I often missed meetings. I eventually had to get into the habit of looking at the posted notes every morning when I got into work. Now, as soon as I sit down at my desk, I look at the yellow scraps of paper and see what I have to do that day.

Self-Advocacy Skills

One of the biggest problems that I have with most special education programs is that they make students with disabilities become dependent on other people. That is, high school students with learning disabilities are so used to having people advocate for them that they often don't know how to advocate for themselves. For example, as a high school teacher, I got formal letters from special education teachers telling me that such and such student needed this modification or that accommodation.

As a college professor, I don't get any letters. If my students need help or extra time to take a test, they have to tell me. But most don't until it is too late. They show up the day of the test and tell me that they have a learning disability and need to take the exam in a quiet room. Worse yet, they never tell me that they have a learning disability, and they struggle in my class because they didn't get the help that they needed in order to succeed.

By the time a student exits high school, he should be able to walk up to a teacher, explain that he has a learning disability, and politely request accommodations. Furthermore, he should know exactly what kind of accommodations he will need.

Students frequently come up to me and say, "I have a learning disability. I need help with this class." When I ask them what kind of help they need, they merely shrug their shoulders. They haven't a clue about what supports they require. Please, make sure that your child learns what kinds of modifications or accommodations she requires.

Also teach your child how to politely and professionally advocate for himself. I have had many students demand help. Although they are certainly entitled to it, being rude and threatening to sue me if I don't give them what they need isn't going to endear them to me or any other teacher and future boss.

Self-Awareness

The next skill that your child needs to succeed in adult life is self-awareness. This goes along with what I was just talking about, but it bears repeating.

For your child to be able to advocate for herself, she has to understand when, where, and how she learns best. She has to know what kind of learning difficulties she has and how to avoid or minimize them. Furthermore, by the time your child gets to college or the work world, she should have an arsenal of strategies that will help her learn effectively.

Again, many of my college students with learning disabilities don't even know what kind of learning disabilities they have. When I ask them what kind of help they need, they don't know. How can they learn effectively if they don't understand their own needs? How can they accomplish the things that they want to accomplish?

My point is this: Make sure that your child understands what a learning disability is. Make sure that he understands how his learning disability affects him. Explain to him why he is given various accommodations and why his teachers use certain teaching strategies.

Your child should be part of the IEP process. She should be aware of what is going on and why. When she leaves high school, she should be able to learn effectively on her own or have the self-advocacy skills needed to get the accommodations that she requires. Otherwise, her entire 12 years in school would have been a huge waste of time.

Self-Initiation

I clearly remember my first day at college. The professor came into the room and said coldly, "I don't care if you come to class. I don't care if you do the assignments or the readings. I am not here to hold your hands or wipe your noses."

I remember thinking, "This is going to be great!" I went to class whenever I felt like it. I didn't read all of the chapters. I basically did whatever I wanted. As a result, I nearly failed out of school my first year.

I think that the hardest thing for many of my students with learning disabilities to do is to take initiative. They seem to have problems doing things on their own. If someone doesn't tell them to do something, such as attend class, read a chapter, or do an assignment, they don't do it. Furthermore, when they have a big project or paper due, they often wait until the last moment to start working on it.

To be successful in the adult world, your child needs to be able to self-initiate activities. If he wants to go to college, he will have to fill out the forms and apply. If he wants to get a job, he will have to develop a résumé and show up on time for interviews. The days of having a special education teacher looking over his shoulder, making sure that he does everything, are over.

Because students in special education often become dependent on people telling them what to do, I recommend that parents and teachers begin fading this support soon after the child enters high school. I encourage teachers and parents to develop the "natural consequences" philosophy. That is, rather than constantly remind students to do their homework, read the assigned chapters, and so forth, they should tell students only once. If they don't do it, they fail the assignment. If they fail too many assignments, they fail the class and have to take it over during the summer.

It may sound harsh, but if your child can't do things without constantly being reminded, he won't do well in college or the adult world. After all, it isn't as if the IRS is going to call and say to your adult child, "Hey, Susie, I just want to remind you to pay your taxes this year." Nor will the water, power, and phone companies call repeatedly either. To be successful, your child has to be able to take the initiative and do things without being told. This takes practice, and the practice must start before your child graduates high school.

EMPLOYMENT ISSUES

Unfortunately, adults with learning disabilities tend to have significant problems in the workforce. They are far more likely to be unemployed than their nondisabled peers. Moreover, they are far more likely to be underemployed; that is, they are far more likely to work at part-time and low-paying jobs than their nondisabled peers are.

The reasons for these vocational difficulties aren't the learning disabilities themselves. After all, people with learning disabilities can be productive citizens. They can learn marketable skills and be valuable employees.

The reasons why many adults with learning disabilities have vocational difficulties are attributed to the issues that I have already talked about in this chapter and throughout the entire book. Adults with learning disabilities are not typically self-motivated. They don't take risks. They aren't self-aware, and they don't know how to affectively advocate for themselves. They tend to be passive learners who don't keep their skills in line with what their employers require. Consequently, they tend to be expendable or, at the very least, passed over for promotions.

For your child to be successful in the work world, she has to learn these skills. She has to learn how to be a self-starter. She has to take risks and advocate for herself. She has to be organized, understand her strengths and weaknesses, and constantly update her skills. But there are other crucial factors as well.

For instance, your child will have to find a job that matches his skills and interests. He could be a self-starting, highly motivated, educated, and organized person, but if he finds himself in a job that he hates, chances are that he won't last very long. Without the proper job match, people with and without learning disabilities are doomed to be miserable for most of their working lives.

As I discuss when talking about finding the right major, I strongly recommend that young adults with learning disabilities meet with vocational counselors. They can help your child determine what kinds of jobs are out there that might match her needs, interests, and skills. Moreover, they can even help your child prepare her résumé, practice interviewing, and find employers who are hiring.

While we are on the topic of employment, we better cover ADA, the American's With Disabilities Act, at least briefly. You see, many people erroneously believe that ADA guarantees people with disabilities a job, that it protects them from getting fired, and that it forces employers to provide accommodations to workers with disabilities. None of this is true.

As with any legal topics, it is difficult to discuss ADA in only a few paragraphs. So you might want to examine some of the resources that are listed in the back. Several books and websites can help you. However, ADA basically prohibits employers from discriminating against qualified employees who have disabilities. Furthermore, under ADA, employers need only provide "reasonable accommodations."

So even though a job applicant might have a disability, he can still be turned away because he isn't qualified to perform the job's essential functions. Moreover, even if someone with a learning disability is hired, he is not guaranteed every possible accommodation, just reasonable ones.

FINAL SUMMARY

So, here we are at the very end of the book. It has been roughly 5 weeks since I stood outside an elementary school auditorium listening in horror as a gaggle of women tried to convince some poor mother that her son with a learning disability wouldn't make anything out of his life. I asked the mother to contact me, but thus far she hasn't.

I often sit in my office wondering how she and her son are doing. I wonder whether she feels hopeless over her son's future. I wonder whether her son understands who he is or how he learns. I wonder how their lives will turnout.

The thought of their situation, and the situations of many families with children who learn differently, depresses me. There is so much talent out there that is underutilized because of people's misguided perceptions. Think of all of the people with learning disabilities who made valuable contributions to the world. I mean, where would science be if Einstein never took the risk to publish his theories? Where would our country be if John F. Kennedy, Dwight D. Eisenhower, and Woodrow Wilson never ran for public office? How boring would our lives be if people like John Lennon, Robin Williams, Tom Cruise, Bill Cosby, Henry Winkler, and Cher didn't pursue their dreams of being entertainers? Where would I be if I listened to those of my teachers who said that I wasn't "college material" or that I didn't have "what it takes" to be a writer? All of these people have learning disabilities, and they all made a valuable contribution to the world, as can any child.

I hope that you have learned a great many things in our brief time to-gether. I hope that you understand what learning disabilities are and that there are many kinds of them. Furthermore, I hope you understand that how you help your child depends largely on what kind of learning disability he or she has.

Most important, I hope that you understand that learning disabilities aren't bad in and of themselves. They aren't a curse from the Dark Ages. They aren't terminal or life threatening. They don't mean that your child or student is "stupid" or that he or she can't learn or will never succeed in life. Learning disabilities don't mean any of this.

Learning disability is simply a term that indicates that a person processes information differently from what is considered the norm. For example, people with dyslexia have a difficult time processing the words on a page. People with dyscalculia have difficulty processing mathematical or logical trains of though. People such as myself have a difficult time processing what they are told. And so forth. It doesn't make us better or worse than anyone else, just different. And that's okay.

RESOURCES

The following are some resources that you might find useful in your quest to help your child. As with everything, please take precaution and judge their merits for yourself based on your own needs.

Mission statements for organizations and descriptions of e-groups come directly from their corresponding websites. All information was current at the time of publication.

BOOKS AND OTHER PRINTED RESOURCES

The following are books and other printed material that you might find useful. I have attempted to organize them into various sections (e.g., books about learning disabilities in general, books about study skills). However, there is considerable overlap between each section. For instance, some books in the general information category might also include information on adult issues. You might want to skim all of the books listed to find what you need.

General Information on Learning Disabilities

Adelizzi, J. U., & Goss, D. B. (2001). *Parenting children with learning disabilities*. Westport, CT: Bergin & Garvey.

Bender, W. N. (2002). *Differentiating instruction for students with learning disabilities: Best teaching practices for general and special educators*. Thousand Oaks, CA: Corwin Press.

Gaddes, W. H., & Edgell, D. (1993). *Learning disabilities and brain function: A neuropsychological approach* (3rd ed.). New York: Springer.

Glenchur, K. E. (2003). *Learning disabilities from a parent's perspective: What you need to know to understand, help, and advocate for your child*. San Francisco: Pince-Nez Press.

Harwell, J. M. (2002). *Complete learning disabilities handbook: Ready-to-use strategies and activities for teaching students with learning disabilities* (2nd ed.). San Francisco: Jossey-Bass.

Lerner, J. W. (2003). *Learning disabilities: Theories diagnosis and teaching strategies* (9th ed.). Boston: Houghton Mifflin.

Mooney, J., & Cole, D. (2000). *Learning outside the lines*. New York: Simon & Schuster.

Smith, C., & Strick, L. (1999). *Learning disabilities: A to Z: A parent's complete guide to learning disabilities from preschool to adulthood*. New York: Free Press.

Swanson, H. L., Harris, K. R., & Graham, S. (2003). *Handbook of learning disabilities*. New York: Guilford Press.

Wong, B. Y. L. (1998) *Learning about learning disabilities* (2nd ed.). San Diego, CA: Academic Press.

Information on Special Education and Special Education Law

Anderson, W., Chitwood, S., & Hayden, D. (1997). *Negotiating the special education maze: A guide for parents and teachers* (3rd ed.). Bethesda, MD: Woodbine House.

Cimera, R. E. (2003). *The truth about special education: A guide for parents and teachers*. Lanham, MD: ScarecrowEducation.

Gargiulo, R. M. (2005). *Special education in contemporary society: Introduction to exceptionality* (2nd ed.). Belmont, CA: Wadsworth.

Havelock, R. C., & Hamilton, J. L. (2003). *Guiding change in special education: How to help schools with new ideas and practices.* Thousand Oaks, CA: Corwin Press.

Kauffman, J. M., & Hallahan, D. P. (2004). *Special education: What it is and why we need it.* Boston: Allyn & Bacon.

Murdick, N. L., Gartin, B. C., & Crabtree, T. L. (2001). *Special education law.* Upper Saddle River, NJ: Prentice Hall.

Smith, D. D. (2003). *Introduction to special education: Teaching in an age of opportunity* (5th ed.). Boston: Allyn & Bacon.

Stowe, C. M. (2005). *Understanding special education: A helpful handbook for classroom teachers.* Washington, DC: Teaching Strategies.

Wilmhurst, L., & Brue, A. W. (2005). *A parent's guide to special education: Insider advice on how to navigate the system and help your child succeed.* New York: AMACOM.

Wright, P. W. D., & Wright, P. (2006). *Wrightslaw: From emotions to advocacy: The special education survival guide.* Hartfield, VA: Harbor House Law Press.

Yell, M. L. (2005). *The law and special education* (2nd ed.). Upper Saddle River, NJ: Prentice Hall.

Information on Study Skills, Preparing for College, and Adult Life

Basili, S., & Zeitlin, J. (2004). *Kaplan ACT 2005.* New York: Kaplan.

Berger, L., Colton, M., Mistry, M., Rossi, P., Xu, J., & Rossi, P. (1998). *Up your score: The underground guide to the SAT: Revised for 2005–2006.* New York: Workman.

College Board. (2004). *The official SAT study guide: For the new SAT.* New York: Author.

Dolber, R. (1996). *College and career success for students with learning disabilities.* New York: McGraw-Hill.

Fast, Y. (2004). *Employment for individuals with Asperger syndrome or non-verbal learning disability: Stories and strategies.* Philadelphia: Jessica Kingsley.

Fiske, E. B., & Hammond, B. G. (2004). *Fiske guide to getting into the right college* (2nd ed.). Naperville, IL: Sourcebooks.

Lurie, K., Pecsenye, M., & Robinson, A. (2005). *Cracking the GRE, with CD-ROM.* New York: Princeton Review.

Martz, G., Magloire, K., & Silver, T. (2005). *Cracking the ACT, with sample tests on CD-ROM.* New York: Princeton Review.

Peterson's. (2003). *Colleges for students with learning disabilities or ADD (Peterson's colleges with programs for students with learning disabilities or attention deficit disorders)* (7th ed). Lawrenceville, NJ: Author.

Robinson, A., & Katzman, J. (2005). *Cracking the NEW SAT, 2006.* New York: Princeton Review.

Spaihts, J., & Sultan, G. (2005). *Cracking the SAT Math 1 and 2 subject tests* (Rev. ed.). New York: Princeton Review.

Strichart, S. S., & Mangrum, C. T. (2001). *Teaching study skills and strategies to students with learning disabilities, attention deficit disorders, or special needs* (3rd ed.). Boston: Allyn & Bacon.

Wax, I. F., & Kravets, M. (2003). *K & W guide to colleges for students with learning disabilities or attention deficit disorder* (7th ed.). New York: Princeton Review.

ORGANIZATIONS AND SUPPORT GROUPS

Association on Higher Education and Disability

AHEAD is the premiere professional association committed to full participation of persons with disabilities in postsecondary education. AHEAD dynamically addresses current and emerging issues with respect to disability, education, and accessibility to achieve universal access.
P.O. Box 540666,
Waltham, MA 02454 USA
Phone: (781) 788-0003
Fax: (781) 788-0033
Website: http://www.ahead.org/

Council for Exceptional Children

The worldwide mission of the Council for Exceptional Children is to improve educational outcomes for individuals with exceptionalities.
1110 North Glebe Road, Suite 300
Arlington, VA 22201-5704

Phone: (888) CEC-SPED (232-7733)
Website: http://www.cec.sped.org

Council for Learning Disabilities
The Council for Learning Disabilities is an international organization that promotes evidence-based teaching, collaboration, research, leadership, and advocacy. CLD is composed of professionals who represent diverse disciplines and are committed to enhancing the education and quality of life for individuals with learning disabilities and others who experience challenges in learning.
P.O. Box 40303
Overland Park, KS 66204
Phone: (913) 492-8755
Fax: (913) 492-2546
Website: http://www.cldinternational.org/

International Dyslexia Association
The International Dyslexia Association is a non-profit organization dedicated to helping individuals with dyslexia, their families, and the communities that support them. IDA is the oldest learning disabilities organization in the nation—founded in 1949 in memory of Dr. Samuel T. Orton, a distinguished neurologist. Throughout our rich history, our goal has been to provide the most comprehensive forum for parents, educators, and researchers to share their experiences, methods, and knowledge.
Chester Building, Suite 382
8600 LaSalle Road
Baltimore, Maryland 21286-2044 USA
Phone: (410) 296-0232
Fax: 410-321-5069
Website: http://www.interdys.org/

Learning Disabilities Association
LDA is dedicated to identifying causes and promoting prevention of learning disabilities and to enhancing the quality of life for all individuals with learning disabilities and their families by encouraging effective identification and intervention, fostering research, and protecting their rights under the law. LDA seeks to accomplish this through awareness, advocacy, empowerment, education, service, and collaborative efforts.

4156 Liberty Road, Suite 1
Pittsburgh, PA 15234-1349
Phone: (412) 341-1515
Fax: (412) 344-0224
Website: http://www.ldaamerica.org/

Learning Disabilities Worldwide
Learning Disabilities Worldwide works to enhance the lives of individuals with learning disabilities, with a special emphasis on the underserved. Our purpose is to identify and support the unrecognized strengths and capabilities of persons with learning disabilities. We strive to increase awareness and understanding of learning disabilities through our multilingual media productions and publications that serve populations across cultures and nations. Our educational enrichment programs are designed to serve individuals with learning disabilities, their families, and the professionals in their lives.
P.O. Box 142
Weston, MA 02493
Phone: (781) 890-LDWW (5399)
Fax: (781) 890-0555
Website: http://www.ldworldwide.org/

National Association for Adults With Special Learning Needs
NAASLN is an association for those who serve adults with special learning needs. NAASLN members include educators, trainers, employers and human service providers.
c/o Correctional Education Association
8182 Lark Brown Rd., Suite 202
Elkridge, MD 21075
Phone: (800) 496-9222
Website: http://www.naasln.org/

National Association for the Education of African American Children With Learning Disabilities
The National Association for the Education of African American Children With Learning Disabilities was founded in 1999 for the purpose of

increasing awareness and promoting an understanding of the specific issues facing African American children. The organization's mission is to
link information and resources provided by an established network of
individuals and organizations experienced in minority research and special education with parents, educators, and others responsible for providing a quality education for all students.
P.O. Box 09521
Columbus, Ohio 43209
Phone: (614) 237-6021
Fax: (614) 238-0929
Website: http://www.charityadvantage.com/aacld/HomePage.asp

National Center for Learning Disabilities
The National Center for Learning Disabilities works to ensure that the
nation's 15 million children, adolescents and adults with learning disabilities have every opportunity to succeed in school, work and life.
NCLD provides essential information to parents, professionals and individuals with learning disabilities, promotes research and programs to
foster effective learning, and advocates for policies to protect and
strengthen educational rights and opportunities.
381 Park Avenue South Suite 1401
New York, NY 10016
Phone: (212) 545-7510, (888) 575-7373
Fax: (212) 545-9665
Website: http://www.ncld.org/

National Coalition on Auditory Processing Disorders
The mission of the National Coalition on Auditory Processing Disorders
is to assist families and individuals affected by auditory processing dis-
orders through education, support, and public awareness as well as pro-
moting auditory access of information for those affected by auditory
processing disorders.
Attn: Membership
P.O. Box 494
Rockville Centre, NY 11571-0494
Website: http://www.ncapd.org/php/

National Dissemination Center for Children With Disabilities
We serve the nation as a central source of information on disabilities in
infants, toddlers, children, and youth; IDEA, which is the law authoriz-
ing special education; No Child Left Behind (as it relates to children
with disabilities); and research-based information on effective educa-
tional practices.
P.O. Box 1492
Washington, DC 20013
Phone: (800) 695-0285
Fax: (202) 884-8441
Website: http://www.nichcy.org/

National Institute on Child Health and Human Development
The mission of the NICHD is to ensure that every person is born
healthy and wanted, that women suffer no harmful effects from repro-
ductive processes, and that all children have the chance to achieve their
full potential for healthy and productive lives, free from disease or dis-
ability, and to ensure the health, productivity, independence, and well-
being of all people through optimal rehabilitation.
P.O. Box 3006
Rockville, MD 20847
Phone: (800) 370-2943
Fax: (301) 984-1473
Website: http://www.nichd.nih.gov/

E-GROUPS

E-groups are online communities where people with similar interests e-
mail each other, sharing resources and experiences. Please keep in mind
that the content offered via these groups is often unmonitored. However, they can be a great source of support.

All of the following groups are from yahoo.com. Other groups exist
from other Internet service providers.

Dyslexia Club
This club is for the discussion of dyslexia and related topics.
Website: http://health.groups.yahoo.com/group/dyslexiaclub/

Dyslexia Support
This list is for the discussion of dyslexia.
Website: http://groups.yahoo.com/group/DyslexiaSupport/

Education-a-Must
Education-a-Must provides advocate services for the child or youth with physical, emotional, behavioral, or learning disabilities. Our goal is to assist parents and caregivers in finding help for the child with special needs.
Website: http://groups.yahoo.com/group/educationamust/

Gifted but Learning Disabled
The purpose of this group is to discuss issues in education for students who have been identified as gifted or who have gifted potential but who also have learning disabilities.
Website: http://groups.yahoo.com/group/gifted_but_learning_disabled/

Global Health Network
International support community for people affected by dyslexia.
Website: http://groups.yahoo.com/group/dyslexia/

Homeschooling Special Needs Children
Our focus is on homeschooling families with at least one special needs child.
Website: http://groups.yahoo.com/group/special-needs-homeschool/

Homeschool Special Needs Kidz
Whether your child has ADHD, a learning disability, dyslexia, emotional or neurological disorder, bipolar, tourette syndrome, deafness, autism, anxiety disorder, oppositional defiance disorder, blindness, any type of emotional or physical handicap, then this group is for you.
Website: http://groups.yahoo.com/group/Homeschool_SpecialNeedsKidz/

Kids With Learning Disabilities
As the mother of three children with learning disabilities, I wanted a place where others can share their experiences. Doctors, educators, and parents are encouraged to join and share their experiences.
Website: http://groups.yahoo.com/group/kidswithlearningdisabilities/

Learning Abled Kids

LA Kids is an advice/support group for parents who are homeschooling their bright children who happen to have learning difficulties. This group has a related resource website, http://www.learningabledkids .com/.
Website: http://groups.yahoo.com/group/LearningAbledKids/

Learning Disabled Action Network

The Learning Disabled Action Network's purpose is to inform people with learning disabilities of their legal rights and what to do if they are violated.
Website: http://groups.yahoo.com/group/learningdisabledactionnetwork/

Reed Martin SPED Law

Reed Martin Special Education Advocacy Strategies and Resources. Assisting parents and advocates in special education advocacy for children with disabilities.
Website: http://groups.yahoo.com/group/ReedMartinSPEDlaw/

Specific Learning Abilities

This support group is to help parents and professionals learn how to help children who have specific learning abilities.
Website: http://health.groups.yahoo.com/group/learningabilities/

REFERENCES

Bender, W. N. (2004). *Learning disabilities: Characteristics, identification, and teaching strategies*. Boston: Allyn & Bacon.

Breitt's version of brain basics. (n.d.). Retrieved April 16, 2007, from http://www.american.edu/kbreitt/home/brain.html

Centers for Disease Control and Prevention. (2006). *Fetal alcohol spectrum disorders*. Retrieved April 16, 2007, from http://www.cdc.gov/ncbddd/fas/fasask.htm#how

Child Development Institute. (2006). *Famous people with attention deficit and learning disorders*. Retrieved May 11, 2007, from http://www.childdevelopmentinfo.com/disorders/famous.shtml

Clickmazes. (2000). *Maze gallery*. Retrieved April 16, 2007, from http://www.clickmazes.com/mazes/ixmaze.htm

Cycleback.com. (2005). Is it a vase or is it two faces? In *Aesthetics, subjectivity, and false realities*. Retrieved April 16, 2007, from http://www.cycleback.com/resonance.html

Funch, F. (1995). The meaning of perception. In *Transformational dialogues*. Van Nuys, CA: Transformational Processing Institute. Retrieved April 16, 2007, from http://www.worldtrans.org/TP/TP1/TP1-9.HTML

Individuals With Disabilities Education Improvement Act, Pub. L. No. 108-446 (2004).

Jergen, R. (2004). *The little monster: Growing up with ADHD*. Lanham, MD: ScarecrowEducation.

Learning Disabilities Association of America. (2007). *Learning disabilities and low income populations.* Pittsburgh, PA: Author.

Morphonix. (2006). *Neuron parts.* Retrieved April 16, 2007, from http://www .morphonix.com/software/education/science/brain/game/specimens/neuron_ parts.html

National Center for Education Statistics. (2006). *Dropout rates in the United States.* Washington, DC: Author.

National Center on Health Statistics. (2006). Birthweight and gestation. In *Fast stats: A to Z.* Retrieved April 16, 2007, from http://www.cdc.gov/nchs/fastats/ birthwt.htm

Schoolhouse Rock. (n.d.). I'm just a bill. In *Schoolhouse Rock lyrics.* Retrieved April 16, 2007, from http://www.schoolhouserock.tv

Sitlington, P. L., & Clark, G. M. (2006). *Transition education and services for students with disabilities.* Boston: Allyn & Bacon.

Spatial intelligence. (n.d.). Retrieved April 16, 2007, from http://www.ul.ie/ ~mearsa/9519211/newpage2.htm

U.S. Department of Education. (2001). *Twenty-third annual report to Congress on the implementation of the Individual With Disabilities Education Act.* Washington, DC: Author.

U.S. Department of Education. (2002). *Executive summary. Twenty-third annual report to Congress on the implementation of the Individuals With Disabilities Education Act.* Washington, DC: Author.

U.S. Department of Education. (2006). *Twenty-eighth annual report to Congress on implementation of the Individuals With Disabilities Education Act.* Washington, DC: Author.

U.S. Department of Labor. (2006). *Labor earnings projections.* Washington, DC: Author.